I.S. 61 Library

I.S. 61 Library

Martin
Luther
King, Jr.

Young Man with a Dream

By Dharathula H. Millender

Aladdin Paperbacks

Aladdin Paperbacks
An imprint of Simon & Schuster
Children's Publishing Division
1230 Avenue of the Americas
New York, NY 10020
Copyright © 1969, 1983 by the Bobbs-Merrill Company, Inc.
All rights reserved including the right of reproduction
in whole or in part in any form.
First Aladdin Paperbacks edition, 1986
Printed in the United States of America

20
Library of Congress Cataloging-in-Publication Data

Millender, Dharathula H.
    Martin Luther King, Jr. : young man with a dream.

    Reprint. Originally published: Indianapolis : Bobbs-
Merrill, 1969.
    Summary: A biography of the civil rights leader whose
philosophy and practice of nonviolent civil disobedience
helped American blacks win many battles for equal rights.
    1. King, Martin Luther—Childhood and youth—Juvenile
literature.   2. Afro-Americans—Biography—Juvenile
literature.   3. Baptists—United States—Clergy—
Biography—Juvenile literature.   4. Afro-Americans—
Civil rights—Juvenile literature.   [1. King, Martin
Luther.   2. Clergy.   3. Afro-Americans—Biography.
4. Afro-Americans—Civil rights]   I. Fiorentino,
Al, ill.   II. Title.
[E185.97.K5M48   1986]   323.4'092'4[B][92]   86-10739
ISBN 0-02-042010-2

To
My niece Daisy
and my godchildren, Teddy and Sharon

The author wishes to express her appreciation to the following persons for their gracious assistance and encouragement in the preparation of this book: Mr. William Ponder, Mrs. Flossie Jones, Mrs. L. P. Johnson, Mr. W. L. Calloway, Mr. R. H. Wilson, Miss Rebecca Dickerson, Mrs. Sanona Harris, Miss Elizabeth Lemon, Rev. William Holmes Borders and Mrs. Borders, Mr. Jesse Blayton, Rev. Walter McCall, Rev. Larry Williams, Mr. Frederick D. Browne. Also she wishes to thank the Scott family for helpful information and use of the files of the *Atlanta Daily World;* Mr. George W. Lee, Grand Commissioner of Education of the Elks Lodge; Mrs. G. W. Barksdale and Miss Miles of the Atlanta University Library; Mr. John E. Hill, Secretary, Atlanta Elks Lodge; the Atlanta office of the Southern Christian Leadership Conference for the historical booklet on the organization; and Mrs. Christine Farris for making available interesting information on her brother's life.

Finally the author wishes to thank the students of Pulaski Junior High School, Gary, Indiana, for suggesting what children might want to know about the life of Dr. Martin Luther King, Jr.; and her daughter, Naomi, for reading and criticizing the manuscript.

Illustrations

Full pages

Numerous smaller illustrations

Contents

★   ★

Books by Dharathula H. Millender

CRISPUS ATTUCKS: BLACK LEADER OF COLONIAL PATRIOTS

★ # Martin Luther King, Jr.

Young Man with a Dream

A New Leader Is Born

SMACK! went the doctor's hand gently but firmly on the naked buttocks of the newborn baby. The doctor frowned. He was concerned because the newborn baby didn't cry out. The doctor's helpers waited and watched. They were concerned, too, that the baby did not cry out. They wanted to see some sign of life in him.

The doctor gripped the baby's feet more firmly. He held him up and tapped him on the buttocks again. The baby's eyes were closed, but he let out a weak cry. Then he made a stronger cry. The doctor and his helpers seemed relieved. The new baby was alive!

This was January 15, 1929. The place was Atlanta, Georgia. It was a cold, cloudy Tuesday. The baby's father had paced the floor of the 12-room house, waiting for his second child to be born. The house was located at 501 Auburn Avenue near the crest of a hill.

Everything in the big house was spotlessly clean. A bed had been set up in one of the rooms downstairs. Many babies in those days were born in homes rather than hospitals. In fact, few hospitals in any part of the country had beds for Negro mothers. It was expected that Negro babies would be born in the home.

There was a threat of flu in the community. Seven thousand cases had been reported. Great care had been taken to keep flu germs outside the house. The doctor's helpers, who were friends of the family, had bustled about in spotless clothing. They had worked hard, trying to make the mother, Alberta King, comfortable.

When the doctor finally tapped life into the baby, everyone quietly rejoiced. The mother fell asleep, as if exhausted. She smiled as she slept. She had given birth to her first son, but little did she know how great he would become.

The big gray and white house on Auburn Avenue was very attractive. It had a porch that extended across the front and around one side. There were neighboring houses not far away on either side. In front was a yard, which was covered with beautiful grass during the summer. A hedge extended across the front of the yard which was kept neatly trimmed. In the spring and summer pretty flowers bloomed in the yard. There was a very large backyard where the baby would someday play with his family and friends.

Two Christian leaders lived in this big house on Auburn Avenue. One was Alberta King's father and the baby's grandfather, the Rev. Adam Daniel Williams. He was the pastor of

Ebenezer Baptist Church, which was a very large church in Atlanta. The other leader was the baby's father, Rev. Martin Luther King, Sr. He was the assistant pastor of the same church where the baby's grandfather was pastor.

Rev. King had been very quiet as he had walked the floor. He already had a daughter named Christine, who was a little more than a year old. Now he was happy. He had a son, Martin Luther King, Jr., who could follow in his footsteps as a great leader.

The new baby boy was born at the beginning of a great depression. Jobs were scarce and many people were out of work. They had little money to spend and little food to eat.

Negroes were having especially hard times, but the new baby was well cared for. The King family had a place to live, food to eat, and clothes to wear. Rev. Williams, however, had to help many people through his church.

The members of the church looked to Rev. Williams, and he never failed them. He never seemed too tired to work on first one problem and then another. The church had many problems, but it always was filled with joy, too. The singing was full of spirit, and the members were helpful, one to another.

Rev. Williams had begun his leadership in a small church in Atlanta in 1894, just twenty-nine years after the freeing of the slaves. At that time many Negroes were trying to find jobs and places to live. Many left the rural areas and moved into the nearby cities. Some left the South entirely and traveled many hundred miles to cities "up North."

Most Negroes from the Georgia rural areas moved into Atlanta. After they found homes, they looked for nearby churches to attend. Many of them found their way to Rev. Williams' church, which made them welcome. They found friendly members in the church and a capable and dedicated leader who could help them find better ways of living.

The new citizens were looking for better opportunities for their children. They sought someone who would help them make more out of their lives, so they could do more for their children. All in all, they hoped for a better to-morrow.

Day after day and night after night the new-comers filled the benches of Rev. Williams' church. They heard his fiery sermons against the evils of segregation. They listened as he encouraged them to work hard for their own betterment and to stand up for their rights. They believed in his plea for unity among themselves.

Within a few years the church became Ebenezer Baptist Church. More and more people crowded into the church each Sunday. They came to hear Rev. Williams and to find hope and

courage for the coming week. Each and every one of them obtained help from the pastor.

Rev. Williams lived and worked at about the same time as two other famous Negro leaders, Booker T. Washington and Dr. W. E. B. DuBois, both college professors. Booker T. Washington was the head of Tuskeegee Institute in Tuskeegee, Alabama. He taught his students to work hard, mainly with their hands, and urged them not to worry too much about fighting for their rights as citizens.

He felt that if they worked hard, white people ultimately would give them their rights. Then in 1895 he made a famous speech at Atlanta. He encouraged Negroes to make the best of segregated conditions until the conditions could be changed for the better.

The other Negro leader, Dr. W. E. B. DuBois, was a professor at Atlanta University. He agreed with Rev. Williams in believing that Negroes should fight for their rights as citizens. DuBois and Williams felt that Negro citizens should have opportunities to develop their minds as well as learn to use their hands.

At the same time Rev. Williams realized that many members of his church would have to earn a living mainly by using their hands. Many were domestic workers in homes, janitors of buildings, or held other similar jobs. These persons needed to be encouraged to lead the best possible lives on meager means.

By the time Martin Luther King was born, Atlanta had become a great educational center for Negroes. Many teachers had come down from the North to start private schools for Negroes. One of these schools was Atlanta University where Dr. DuBois taught, and another was Spellman Seminary.

Rev. Williams had sent his daughter, Alberta, the new baby's mother, to Spellman Seminary. Afterward he had sent her to Hampton Institute in Virginia. There she had become a school teacher and had taught until her first child, Christine, was born.

There was much unrest about Negroes across the country. Many white people did not seem to understand Negroes. Suddenly, after the War beween the States, a few Negroes had moved into positions of leadership. Some had served in state legislatures and some had even become members of the United States Congress. Some had held other important positions in state and national governments.

This new type of Negro leadership had lasted only a few years. By the time Rev. Williams had started his church, Negroes had ceased to hold such positions of leadership. Most of them had been pushed back almost to the kinds of lives they had led in slavery.

Many people did not want Negroes to get ahead. They did not want Negroes to have good homes or to get an education. They tried to hold Negroes back, by keeping them poor and uneducated. Some even wrote degrading articles about Negroes, which were published in newspapers and magazines. They frequently wrote that Negroes were lazy and didn't want to work for a living. They indicated that Negroes did not care about improving their conditions or about properly caring for their children.

Many readers believed these articles, but Rev. Williams knew they were untrue. He tried to inspire the members of his church to have faith and hope. He encouraged them to work for better conditions, but always to strive to be good citizens.

Finally in 1909 so many problems between whites and Negroes arose across the country, that Negro leaders formed a new national organization, to help protect them from injustices and to help them advance. This new organization was called the National Association for the Advancement of Colored People, NAACP, which was a shorter way of saying the long name. One of the pioneers in forming the new organization was Dr. DuBois of Atlanta University. Another important leader was Rev. Williams.

In Atlanta, under the leadership of Rev Williams, the new organization forced the city to build a Negro public high school. It led Negroes to boycott a newspaper that published degrading articles about Negroes and forced the newspaper to go out of business. Constantly the members of Ebenezer Baptist Church fought for improvement in Negro opportunities.

In 1931, when the new baby Martin Luther King, Jr. was only two years old, his grandfather, Rev. Williams, died. Then Rev. M. L. King, Sr., the baby's father and the son-in-law of Rev. Williams, became the pastor of Ebenezer Baptist Church. Like Rev. Williams, he was a very forceful leader.

Thus, from the very beginning, Martin Luther King, Jr. was born into a life of leadership. As he grew, he learned by example how to guide his people. As he grew, too, he demonstrated special leadership abilities of his own.

Segregation at an Early Age

As MARTIN LUTHER KING, JR. grew older, he became known as M. L. Everyone seemed to use the initials rather than his first name, partly to distinguish him from his father.

Years before there had been a mix-up over his father's first name. He had been called Michael Luther, but he had been named Martin Luther, after a famous preacher, who had lived in Europe many centuries before.

M. L. made friends easily. There was a large backyard behind the King house, about twice as large as two ordinary yards. There was enough room for children to play almost any kind of game. All the while M. L. was growing up, children gathered here to play.

As a little boy, M. L. played with two white boys who lived across the street. The two boys' parents had a grocery store. M. L. and the two boys were inseparable playmates for several years. They liked to play the same games and enjoyed doing the same things.

Finally the white boys were old enough to go to school. They started to a school which only white pupils attended, because Negro and white children were not allowed to attend the same schools. The two boys soon found new playmates at school. Their new friends wanted to know why they lived in a Negro neighborhood. The two boys had never thought about this question before. The idea that one neighborhood might be better than another had never occurred to them until now. They could only wonder.

Many white people owned stores and other

business places in the Negro neighborhood. Most of these people lived over their places of business or in houses close by. Their children regularly played with the Negro children in the neighborhood. Then when they went to school their school friends made fun of them. Soon they began to look down on Negro children.

One day M. L. went across the street to play with the two white boys as he had done for several years, but they were nowhere to be seen. He went into the store to ask their parents about them. Their parents acted strange, and said they couldn't come out to play.

The first day this happened, M. L. thought little of it and went home to play with other friends in his back yard. On succeeding days he tried again, and received the same treatment from the parents. Gradually he came to realize that something was wrong.

At last M. L. asked the parents whether the

boys were sick. They replied coldly that the boys couldn't play with him anymore because they were white and he was colored. At that time he didn't really know what being colored meant. He felt insulted, however, just by the parents' tone of voice in telling him.

He looked at his arms and noted that they were brown. He was puzzled and couldn't understand what being "white" or "colored" really meant. He was so hurt that he cried.

He rushed home to ask his mother what all this meant. She looked at the tears in his eyes, wiped them away, and took him on her lap. Then she told him the history of Negroes in this country, starting with the days of slavery. She explained how slaves lived before the War between the States, and how they had been freed by the Emancipation Proclamation.

"Then Negroes became citizens," she explained to the boy on her lap.

M. L. watched his mother carefully as she unfolded the history of Negroes, leading to some of the problems that presently existed. She tried to explain the divided system of the South, where white children went to white schools and colored children to colored schools. She tried to explain segregation in hotels, restaurants, theaters, and all public places. She explained the signs which could be found everywhere, telling which drinking fountains, lavatories, and waiting rooms could be used by white people and which by colored people.

"These signs do not make certain people any better than others," she told her young son. "Adults sometimes can be cruel and unkind, but often they don't mean to be. Now that the parents of these boys won't let them play with you because you are colored, you can play with Christine and your brother A. D."

Mrs. King emphasized that her son should remember one very important thing. She looked at him firmly and said, "You must always remember that you are as good as anyone."

Losing his two white friends hurt M. L. because he didn't understand. He never forgot this incident and resented segregation from then on. He resented being considered unworthy of associating with others.

M. L. was a very bright boy and soon replaced his old friends with new friends. His mother was interested in his obtaining a good education and wanted him to start to school as early as possible. When he was five years old, she thought he was ready, but the problem was to find a place to send him.

There were no kindergartens in Atlanta in the public schools. The only kindergarten in the city was located on the campus of Atlanta University, but this was a private school already filled with pupils. Most children started to school in the first grade when they were six years old. M. L.'s sister, Christine, was now six years old and had already started to the Younge School.

The first grade teacher at the Younge School was Miss Rebecca Dickerson. Mrs. King was a friend of Miss Dickerson and decided to ask her whether she could make room for M. L. School had been in session several weeks and the room already was crowded with pupils, but Miss Dickerson agreed to take him. She would make room for him somehow.

From the beginning, Miss Dickerson noticed that her new pupil already knew many of the things she was teaching. Soon he began skipping over simple exercises in order to work harder ones. He was eager to learn and waited for more and more work. Soon he had passed the slower pupils in the class, and before long caught up with all the bright pupils. By the end of the term he could read as well as or better than any pupil in the Younge School.

Miss Dickerson was glad to have this bright pupil in her class. She was very proud of him because he was obedient and learned so well. He was happy, too, and soon forgot about the two white playmates he had lost.

Learning to Protest

Rev. KING, the new preacher at Ebenezer Baptist Church, had come from rural Georgia. His father, James Albert King, had been a share-cropper on a plantation about twenty miles from Atlanta. A sharecropper is a person who grows crops on part of a plantation or large farm. He cultivates the land and is supposed to receive a share of the crops for his efforts.

After the slaves were freed by the Emancipation Proclamation, some of the plantation owners were kind to their former slaves. They gave them money and food and the choice of remaining on the land or leaving. If they chose to stay, they could work and receive pay for their labor. If they chose to leave, they could go out on their own to some other place.

Some of the landowners, however, were cruel to their former slaves. They drove them off their plantations without money, food, or any means of caring for themselves and their families. These former slaves immediately had to find ways of earning a living. Sometimes sharecropping was the only thing they could do to keep from starving.

Many former slaves wanted first to get an education. They wanted to learn to read and write and figure as most white people could. They felt that learning the three "R's" would give them real freedom. Without a knowledge of reading, writing, and figuring, they feared they could never get ahead. A few had received a little education while they were slaves, but most of them had no book learning whatever.

After the War between the States, many white men in the South had land but little money. They no longer had slaves to cultivate the land for growing and picking cotton. At the same time, the freed Negroes needed homes and places to work. For these reasons many Negroes became sharecroppers. They lived in small shacks and all members of the family worked.

Each sharecropper borrowed seed and fertilizer from the landowner. He agreed to pay for the seed and fertilizer when he harvested his crops. From time to time during the summer he borrowed money and obtained provisions from the landowner in order to live. Every month he became more and more in debt to the landowner.

At the end of the season, the sharecropper settled with the landowner. After he paid back what he had borrowed, he was supposed to share in the profits. Usually, however, he was told that he had no profits coming. Thus, year after year, he continued to be in debt and had no means of escape. In time, sharecropping simply became another form of slavery.

Rev. King's father, James Albert King, had learned firsthand what sharecropping was like. Each year the landlord had provided his father with a house and had loaned him seed, fertilizer, and sometimes money for food. Then each year after he settled up with the landowner, he had found himself a little more in debt than he had been the year before. All the while he had hoped to own land of his own, but he never had had an opportunity to do so.

Fortunately Rev. King had had an opportunity to go to school even though his father had been a sharecropper. He had attended a plantation school, where he had become a brilliant student. Here, unlike his father before him, he had learned to read, write, and figure.

One day when he was about twelve years old,

he had gone with his father to settle with the landowner at the end of the season. He had listened and watched as the landowner had figured and finally he had heard the landowner say that the cotton had come out even. This meant that his father would not receive a single penny for his work.

All the while young King had been figuring on his own. Finally he had turned to his father and said, "Papa, what about the cotton seed?"

Young King had known that his father should receive $1,000 credit in clear money for cotton seed that had been sold from the cotton grown on the land. His question had made the landowner very angry, and the landowner had tried to kick the boy.

Thus as a boy Rev. King had come to hate a sharecropper's life. He had hated working from sun up to sun down, day after day, year after year with no improvement in living conditions.

All the while his family had lived in a shack and had had little to eat and wear.

The boy couldn't make much sense out of this kind of living. As he learned more in school, he had decided that he would have a much greater opportunity in a city. Finally when he was fifteen years old, he had left his father's home, such as it was, and walked twenty miles to the city of Atlanta.

In Atlanta, young King had found it hard to obtain a job. He had worked at several jobs, hauling freight and stoking engines in a railroad yard. At night he had gone to school. Sometimes he could scarcely keep awake, but he had been determined to get an education.

He was twenty-six years old when he had finished high school, but he had kept on studying. Five years later he had finished Morehouse College, which was in Atlanta.

About this time he had become a Baptist

preacher at two small churches in Atlanta. Soon afterward he had met Rev. Williams, who had liked him and felt that he would become a great spiritual leader among his people. Also, he had met Rev. Williams' daughter, with whom he had fallen in love.

Finally he had asked Rev. Williams if he could marry his daughter. The father had consented, and they had been married on Thanksgiving Day in 1926. Then in 1931 Rev. Williams died, and Rev. M. L. King, Sr. became the pastor of the family church.

Rev. King proved to be an excellent successor to his father-in-law. He remembered the many injustices he had witnessed in childhood and was not afraid to speak out. He remembered his many unhappy experiences as a sharecropper's son and realized that many members of his church had had similar experiences. He was determined that they should have opportunities to

lead better lives in the future. He struck back at injustices and made people respect him.

One day Rev. King took M. L. downtown to buy a new pair of shoes. They sat down in the empty seats near the front of the store. Soon a white clerk came up and explained that he couldn't wait on them there. They would have to move to the back of the store.

"There's nothing wrong with these seats," Rev. King told the clerk calmly. "We're quite comfortable here."

Flustered, the young clerk said, "I'm sorry, but you'll have to move."

Rev. King became aggravated by the insult. He had come here to buy shoes and wanted to be treated the same as any other cash customer. Accordingly he snapped back at the clerk, "We'll either buy shoes sitting here, or we won't buy shoes at all."

On second thought Rev. King decided to leave the store at once. He took M. L. by the hand and stalked out of the store. Humiliated and angry, he walked down the street muttering to himself. M. L. walked along beside him, listening closely to what he said. He was particularly interested when he overheard his father say, "I don't care how long I have to live with this system, I will never accept it."

40

Not long after that, M. L. saw his father refuse to accept another insult. They were driving along the street in an automobile, when Rev. King accidentally drove past a stop sign. A policeman immediately pulled up to the automobile and said bluntly, "All right, boy, pull over and let me see your license."

Rev. King pulled over as directed, but proudly and indignantly looked the policeman straight in the eye. "I'm no boy," he said, pointing to M. L. sitting quietly beside him. "This is a boy. I'm a man. Until you call me one, I will not listen to you."

The policeman was shocked, because he had expected the Negro to be submissive. He had not expected a Negro to stand up for his rights. Nervously he wrote up the ticket and left as soon as possible.

All these experiences with his father had great influence on M. L. He noted the injustices that

Negroes suffered day after day, and could understand his father's determination to fight these injustices. He realized that his father had started life, suffering injustices as a sharecropper's son. Now he was proud that his father had become a great spiritual leader, eager to bring justice to his followers.

Teacher's Helper

M. L. GREW up in the church. Everything his family did had to do with the church in some way. As minister of the church, his father was an active member of the Baptist Ministers Union. He worked actively with the Atlanta NAACP and led many fights for first class citizenship for Negroes in the community.

From the pulpit of Ebenezer Baptist Church, M. L. heard plans for the improvement of conditions for Negroes in Atlanta. The NAACP opened a school on the campus of Atlanta University to teach Negroes how to make use of their right to vote. This school which offered a six-week course, was taught by a professor named Rayford Logan. Members of Ebenezer were encouraged to take this six-week course.

Negro leaders, through the NAACP, led a fight on the residential segregation law in Atlanta. This law gave the city clerk the right to keep Negroes from moving into decent housing areas. If the clerk did not give a Negro a permit to move, he could not do so. In this way Negroes were kept from buying houses in other parts of the city. Sometimes, when Negroes obtained permits, their homes were bombed. The NAACP tried to stop such cruelty.

Rev. King regularly urged his members to trade with Negro business men and women. He encouraged them to use their own doctors and lawyers, and to put their money in a Negro bank. He pointed out many opportunities from the pulpit and urged Negroes to help one another in every way they could.

M. L. was proud of his father's leadership and noted that even though he fought for the rights of Negroes, he was highly respected by the whites. He was popular with the white ministers of the city and never was attacked physically as he went about his work.

Rev. King's policy was to attack evil directly. He refused to ride city buses, after he witnessed a brutal attack on a group of Negro passengers. He led a fight to give Negro teachers equal salaries with whites. He objected to the "Jim Crow" elevator in the courthouse, resulting in a change of regulations so that all passengers could ride the same elevators.

M. L. thought about all the action within the church and community. Protest and fighting for rights gradually became a part of his life. Also he was filled with a great hatred of segregation which he saw all about him.

As a boy, M. L. liked music and had a good

voice for singing. His mother, who was an accomplished organist and choir leader, often took him to various churches to sing. Many people came out to hear him sing, "I Want to Be More and More Like Jesus." Later, he became a member of the junior choir in his church.

When M. L. entered the fifth grade in school he attended Mrs. Harris' room in the Howard School. The room was crowded with children seated at desks bolted to the floor. Each desk was flat across the top with an open shelf for storing books and supplies. It had an inkwell on the right side near the front edge. Beside the inkwell was a groove for pencils or pens. The children used stick pens that they dipped into the inkwell as they wrote.

During the first week of school, M. L. demonstrated ability and leadership. Mrs. Harris gave him a job of passing out pens at the beginning of the penmanship lesson. Then at the end of the lesson, he gathered up the pens, counted them, put them away again.

Some of the children in the crowded room were restless and noisy, but M. L. always was very quiet. He never gave any trouble, but laughed occasionally when something funny happened. He liked his studies in school.

Mrs. Harris taught all the different subjects in her room, arithmetic, geography, English, writing, science, and spelling. M. L. liked arithmetic best, especially fractions, but he also was good in reading and spelling.

All the pupils in the room were grouped according to their ability to learn. M. L. learned so fast that he always seemed to need something more to do. Finally Mrs. Harris thought of using him as a helper, but she was puzzled at first about what she should ask him to do.

One day she asked him to help a slow group of pupils in arithmetic to learn fractions. Almost at

once, without practice, he became a good helping teacher. He liked the pupils and they liked
him. He was patient with them and took time to
go over the exercises time after time. Frequently
he rewarded them with such words as "very
good" and "excellent" and encouraged them
constantly to "try a little harder."

Mrs. Harris' children enjoyed spelling bees in
which two teams spelled against each other.
When a child missed a word, he had to drop out
of his team. The contest continued until only
the best speller on each team was left. M. L.
nearly always was one of the winners. He was
an excellent speller and was filled with a desire
to win.

Often a boys' team spelled against a girls'
team. One day Mrs. Harris asked M. L. to
choose a boys' team while she chose a girls' team.
He took so much time that she wondered what
he was doing. Then she smiled, because she

found that he was trying to give every boy the best possible chance. At the same time he was trying to find the best possible spellers.

When Mrs. Harris taught social studies, she often allowed her pupils to select famous people from the lesson and portray them for the class. The pupils put on class programs in which they recited addresses which famous people had given or poems which famous people had written. On these occasions M. L , whenever possible, selected Abraham Lincoln. Then he would recite Lincoln's Gettysburg Address.

When M. L. went forward to give Lincoln's Address he would hold his head high and his eyes would take on a special gleam. Then he would start in with a strong melodious voice, "Fourscore and seven years ago our fathers brought forth on this continent a new nation, conceived in liberty, and dedicated to the proposition that all men are created equal . . ."

M. L. thought the first part of the speech had the most meaning, but the class always enjoyed the whole address. They clapped him back again and again. He enjoyed their attention, but never let it give him false pride. Mrs. Harris decided that he was a born speaker.

Once when the class was studying how the American colonies were seeking independence from England, M. L. chose to act the part of Patrick Henry. He pretended that he was at a church and had to interrupt a church program to tell the audience something important. He explained that the American colonists would have to fight or they never would be free. He explained that they would have to band together and take up arms. Then he closed by reciting Patrick Henry's famous words, "I know not what course others may take; but as for me, give me liberty or give me death!"

When the lessons on famous people were over,

M. L. remembered that his father had told him he was named after a famous person, Martin Luther. He went to the library to find a book on this famous man.

M. L. had a close friend, Willie Ponder, who also was a relative by marriage. His mother had married Rev. King's brother. Willie, M. L. and his younger brother, A. D., were constant companions. Willie was a good listener. One day M. L. told Willie about Martin Luther.

"Willie, did you know that I was named for a famous person?" M. L. asked.

Willie admired M. L. and thought that he had great ability for a boy. Also he thought that some day he would become a famous person, but didn't know that M. L. was named after a famous person. "No, I didn't know," he said. "Tell me who the famous person was."

Martin started to explain. "He was Martin Luther," he said. "My father told me about him many years ago. People just call me M. L. for short. Well, I was reading about him, and he was great. Some of what I read, however, I don't quite understand. I asked the librarian to help me with some of the words. Do you want to hear about him?" he asked.

"Yes, tell me what you found out in the library," Willie replied.

"Martin Luther was a preacher and a leader like my father," said M. L. "He lived many years ago in Europe. He was born in 1483."

"That was really a long time ago," said Willie in an awed voice. "What made him a leader in those days?"

"Well, he was a priest," replied M. L. "The church was all one kind in those days. Everyone went to the Catholic Church, which spread over many countries of Europe. There was a leader over all the Catholic Churches, called the Pope. The Pope was very important."

"It sounds confusing to me," said Willie. "What made M. L. important?"

"He wasn't called M. L., but by his whole name, Martin Luther," said M. L. "He was a preacher in a church. He told his church members how to lead better lives. He told them that God would help them to be better persons, if they trusted in him. But they would have to believe that God would help them, and He would. This was called faith."

"That's no different from what your father preaches," said Willie, even more puzzled. He couldn't see what was so great about asking people to have faith in God to help them live better lives. He heard that every Sunday at the Ebenezer Baptist Church.

"In the old church, members didn't actually read the Bible and didn't know that faith in God would help them," explained M. L. "They contributed money to help build finer churches and

thought this would help them be better persons. They thought that only the Pope could help them. Martin Luther was so upset that he rebelled against the Pope and the church."

"What does rebel mean?" asked Willie.

"It means to fuss about something so loudly that other people come to see what is wrong, too," answered M. L.

"What happened to Martin Luther when he started to fuss in that way?" asked Willie.

"The Pope wanted him to say he was sorry, but he wouldn't, so he had to leave the church," said M. L. "Then he started a church of his own which people called the Lutheran Church."

"Is there a Lutheran Church here in Atlanta?" asked Willie.

"I don't know," said M. L., "but when Martin Luther broke away from the old church, he started something called the Reformation. Many different kinds of churches sprang up all because of the Reformation." He copied the word on a piece of paper and handed it to Willie.

"That's a big word," said Willie, "but I'm going to try to find out more about it. We'll talk about it again tomorrow."

Both boys started to walk home, but Willie still didn't quite understand Martin Luther's great contribution to the world. He was sure, however, that he must have been a great man, if M. L. thought he was.

Living and Learning

M. L. WAS small for his age and big bullies often picked on him when his brother A. D. was not around. M. L. was a year older than his brother, but his brother was taller and huskier than he. M. L. was not a coward, but he couldn't see any sense in fighting.

To M. L. there was something degrading about fighting. He felt that it was shameful for persons to scratch or cut one another, throw rocks at one another, or hit one another with sticks or clubs. According to his way of thinking, handling differences in these ways never settled anything. They only proved that one person was stronger than another or that he could take advantage of another.

Accordingly M. L. always tried to reason with persons, when they thought he had mistreated them. He tried to get them to tell why they had a reason to be angry. Then he tried to convince them, if possible, that he had not intended to harm them in any way.

One day when he was walking along a hall in the library with his arms full of books, he accidentally brushed against a big bully. Politely he said, "Excuse me," and started to walk on. The bully simply followed him outside the building, boasting that he would "take care of" him. M. L. kept on walking, trying to ignore the bully's insulting remarks.

Finally the bully ran in front of M. L. and blocked his path. M. L. was surprised by this brazen move, but managed to inquire, "What do you want?"

The bully laughed loudly and defiantly, but did not answer. By now a crowd had gathered and someone pushed the two boys together, trying to start the fight. Once more M. L. tried to stave off the fight by reasoning.

"What do you want to fight about?" he asked. "In the first place I haven't done anything to you. I brushed into you accidentally. I asked you to pardon me. Now why do you want to mess or tear up our clothes or cause us to get hurt? What will hurting each other prove?"

Several members of the crowd agreed with M. L., but once more someone pushed the two boys together, this time harder than before. Then the fight began. M. L. was badly beaten.

After the fight, the bully and his crowd moved on. Several children stayed to help M. L. get his books together. His feelings were hurt. He said nothing, but he realized that this would never be his way of settling a difference. He would avoid "going to the grass." Instead he would still try to reason things out.

When his brother heard about the fight, he wanted to settle it, but M. L. wouldn't let him. He knew that A. D. could actually defeat the bully, but fighting would settle nothing. It would only make matters worse.

The King brothers shared a bicycle and took turns riding it. M. L. usually took his turn riding in other neighborhoods. He liked to ride around and see how other people lived. Sometimes he rode just to observe and sometimes he stopped to talk with people. Many times he became so interested that he stayed away for hours.

Once when he was riding the bicycle, he had a collision and was brought home bruised with the wrecked bicycle. His brother was very angry when he saw the wrecked bicycle. Then M. L realized how selfish he had been to ride so far from home. From now on he resolved that he would consider other people's wishes and not just his own.

The King family was very close-knit. M. L. was devoted to all the members, including his grandmother, the widow of Rev. Adam Daniel

Williams. When his grandmother died, he felt particularly close to his mother, with whom he shared many secret thoughts.

His mother was a quiet, refined lady, sensitive about the feelings of others. She encouraged M. L. to think only the best of people, and to give them a chance to show their good qualities. His father, on the other hand, was fiery and dynamic, a forceful leader in times of stress and strain. He spoke out loudly and firmly against injustices of every sort.

M. L. was influenced greatly by both his parents and came to act like both of them at times. He usually was quiet and mild-mannered in his actions, yet forceful in his speech, especially when he wanted to get a point across. As he matured, he became more of an observer, a thinker, a reader, and a searcher for truth than anything else.

The King family dinner hour usually was very

busy and interesting. Rev. King would read verses from the Bible before the family enjoyed a well-balanced and delicious meal. Then after the meal was over, he would act as referee while his sons took part in a spirited debate. In this way the sons received practice in thinking and expressing themselves under their father's direction. The entire family enjoyed the arguments, even the mother and sister.

Sunday always was a very busy day in church for the King family. Sunday School was held at 9 a.m. and the preaching service at 11 a.m. Sunday afternoon there usually was some kind of program or special service, and at 6 p.m. there was a meeting of the Baptist Young People's Union (BYPU). Afterwards the regular evening preaching service was held, which was the last meeting of the day. Every member of the family attended all these services. Mrs. King played the organ and directed the choir.

Since Sunday was a busy day, Mrs. King always prepared the Sunday dinner the night before. M. L. stayed up to help her and to keep her company. He fired the furnace, peeled the potatoes, and carried out the garbage. There always was time for conversation, and his mother told him many interesting things about people and life. After M. L. was grown he always remembered these evenings with his mother as one of the best experiences in his life.

Oglethorpe School

GRADUALLY as M. L. became older, more and more people began to call him **Martin** or **Martin Luther King**. Finally while he still was in the higher elementary grades, he was transferred to a private school, known as Oglethorpe Elementary School. This private school was a part of Atlanta University.

Oglethorpe School was rather small. Only about two hundred children attended the school in all the grades from kindergarten through the eighth grade. When children finished the eighth grade, they were admitted to high school without having to take examinations.

Some of the teachers at Oglethorpe were not acquainted with Martin. He was new to them and they treated him as a new pupil. One of his teachers was Miss Lemon, who took a special interest in him. He and Miss Lemon became very close friends.

Martin's parents had to pay tuition for him to attend Oglethorpe. Tuition is a fee charged a person to attend a private or special school. The total tuition for the year was twenty-five dollars, with fifteen dollars payable in the fall of the year and ten dollars payable before the end of January. The tuition covered all the pupil's expenses, including the books, paper, and pencils that he would need.

The Oglethorpe School was a model school, noted for its good teachers. It was a practice school for students in education at Atlanta University. College students who were preparing to become teachers watched the teachers at Oglethorpe School and then practiced teaching there before they graduated.

Children at this school were trained to think for themselves. They were allowed to work as fast or as slowly as they chose. Since all classes were small, most children did very well in their studies.

The two subjects Miss Lemon liked best were social studies and science. In teaching these subjects, she trained her pupils to be honest, self-reliant, and sure of themselves. In addition, she taught them to be good sports. When they pouted because things did not go their way, she took away some of their privileges. Then they could see that pouting didn't pay.

Miss Lemon tried to teach social studies in a very interesting and practical manner. She organized the class as the President's Cabinet in the federal government. Then she acted as President, and the pupils became members of her cabinet. "Without you this government cannot be run properly," she explained.

The pupils liked having a part in classroom government. Every two weeks they held an election, so that each student had a chance to hold different cabinet posts.

The Secretary of State made the telephone calls and the Secretary of the Treasury kept the money. The Secretary of Interior kept the desks and furniture straight. The Secretary of Labor put the paints and brushes and other supplies away in the cabinets.

When the pupils left Miss Lemon's room in the afternoon, she usually said, "Thank you for coming. I'm so glad you came today. Shall I look for you tomorrow?"

The children would smile and say, "Yes, we'll be happy to return tomorrow."

The pupils in the class even punished themselves when they did something wrong. Each pupil would decide how many licks with a ruler he needed to make himself reform. Then he would go to the front of the room, take the ruler in one hand and whack the other hand as many times as he felt was necessary.

One day Martin had to be punished. He was very embarrassed, but he said nothing. He went to the front of the room and stood with the ruler in hand, looking at the silent faces of his classmates. All the pupils were watching.

"If you do not punish yourself well, I will have to do it myself," said Miss Lemon, just as she said to every pupil who was supposed to punish himself.

Martin pressed his lips firmly together and held out one hand. He silently gave himself ten whacks which was the greatest number possible under the rules. Then he quietly replaced the ruler on Miss Lemon's desk, and took his seat. From then on he never needed to punish himself again. Most pupils needed to punish themselves only once. They found it very embarrassing to do so before the class.

Miss Lemon taught the pupils to be independent and to speak out against what they did not feel was right. Everyday she admonished them, "Hold your head up and walk straight."

"You can rebel and still maintain your dignity," she continued. "You do not have to fight with people to show that you do not like what they are doing to you. You can rebel inside, and find quiet ways to show your discontent."

Often in social studies the pupils pretended they were taking imaginary trips around the world and would be gone for the whole year. "Since we will be gone a long time," Miss Lemon would say, "we'll have to let our parents know where we are. How shall we keep in touch with them while we are gone?"

"We can write letters to them," said Martin

confidently. He was very good in writing. He spoke perfect English and could write just as well. When the pupils went on an imaginary world trip, Martin wrote his parents from Egypt.

96 Pyramid Row

Dear Mother and Father,

This is to let you know that we just arrived in Egypt. We are now looking at the pyramid row. We will be leaving here soon and going to the Belgian Congo.

In the Belgian Congo we will see my good friend, Bombo. He will teach us one of the dances of his country.

The houses in his country are not like ours in Atlanta. They are made of leaves and are made so that water runs off the roof.

Please take care of my dog while I am away. I will write you next from the Belgian Congo.

Your loving son,
Martin

Miss Lemon often had reading and story telling periods. Much time during these periods was devoted to Negro history. The pupils read and told many stories about famous Negro heroes. They read many poems and stories actually written by Negro authors.

One story which the children loved was a folk tale called "Little 'Fraid and Big 'Fraid." The pupils never grew tired of reading or telling the story. Martin liked the story and often told it in this way:

"Once upon a time there were two boys who lived on a plantation. Both boys were ten years old. One boy, whose name was Tommy, belonged to the Master of the plantation. The other boy, whose name was Sammy, belonged to a slave who worked on the plantation. Both boys had been good friends and playmates since they first were old enough to play together.

"Each boy had chores to do. Tommy's chore was to pile logs beside the stoves and fireplaces for heating and cooking. This was an important chore. If he didn't keep logs by the stoves and the fireplace, people couldn't keep warm or cook their meals. Sammy's chore was to take the cows out to the field to graze each morning, and to bring them back each evening."

The children greatly enjoyed hearing Martin tell this story. They huddled closer in their circle of chairs, and drew closer to him as he talked. He pressed his lips firmly together, ran his eyes from one listener to another in the circle and continued:

"One evening, about Halloween time, it was getting dark, and neither of the boys had done his chores. The Master called them to him and said, 'Boys, it is getting dark. You have been playing all day and completely forgotten to do your chores.'

"Both boys opened their eyes wide and looked at each other, showing they had forgotten. The Master looked at Sammy and wondered whether he still should send him after the cows. Finally he said, 'Sammy, it's getting so dark. Are you 'fraid to go out now and get the cows?'

"Sammy looked at the Master in a puzzled manner and said, ' 'Fraid? What's 'fraid?'

"The Master realized Sammy wasn't afraid of the dark, so he said, 'That's all right, Sammy. Go on out and get the cows, but hurry back.' Then Sammy picked up the stick which he used for driving the cows from the field and started off to get them.

"At heart Tommy was a mischievous boy. He had taught Sammy many things, but he hadn't taught him to be afraid. So, instead of getting the logs and putting them where they should be, he decided to teach Sammy the meaning of fear.

"Quietly he ran into the bedroom and grabbed a white sheet off the bed. He put the sheet over his head and made holes for two eyes, a nose, and a mouth. Then he swished and danced

74

about in front of the mirror practicing different ways to scare Sammy.

"Now Tommy had a pet monkey, and he failed to notice that the monkey was under the bed watching him. When Tommy dashed out the front door the monkey decided to follow him. The creature grabbed a white pillow case from the bed, put it over his head and made holes for a nose, a mouth, and two big eyes. He practiced swooping about before the mirror just as Tommy had done. Then he swung out the door and hurried along to catch up with Tommy."

By now the group of listeners had moved their chairs still closer until they were almost upon Martin. Even Miss Lemon seemed to enjoy his re-telling of the tale.

"By now Sammy had found the cows," Martin continued, "and was singing as he drove them home with his stick. It was almost dark, but the darkness didn't bother him. He knew his way home, and he walked along driving the cows ahead of him.

"Tommy saw Sammy coming and swung first to the right and then to the left, as he tried to act like a ghost. He shook himself in all sorts of ways, and waved his arms about under the white sheet. Behind him, the monkey did exactly the same things.

"Finally Sammy noticed the two white objects coming down the path. He watched them swooping and swinging about and decided, 'They must be the 'Fraids the Master was talking about.' He stopped to watch.

"Now Tommy tried hard to put on an even better show. He hooted, and jerked, and wheeled, and stomped, and jumped up and down. Then he stood and shook, but Sammy only watched quietly. He didn't seem to act afraid at all by what Tommy was doing. Finally Tommy sat down on a tree stump to think.

76

"The little monkey sat down, too, but on a smaller stump nearby. Tommy crossed his leg and began to swing it, and the monkey did the same thing. Sammy saw both of them but was more interested in the small figure than in the large one. He stared at it.

"Finally Tommy noticed that Sammy was not looking at him but at something else, and he turned to look, too. Then he saw the monkey, but, of course he didn't recognize him under the white pillow case. He just saw something flapping up and down beside him and he jumped up, scared, and began to scream. The monkey did the same.

"By now Tommy was so afraid that he ran to get away from that small white thing. The more he ran, the more the thing ran behind him. He screamed for his mother.

"Sammy thoroughly enjoyed the race. He didn't know what it was all about, but it seemed

like a race between a little white thing and a big white thing. So he jumped up and down and cheered them on and screamed, 'Run, Big 'Fraid, or else Little 'Fraid is going to catch you!' "

When Martin finished his story, the pupils were rocking with laughter. They liked the way he ended the story and showed their enthusiasm by clapping and clapping. He sat quietly down with a smile.

Miss Lemon tried to keep the library well supplied with books about Negroes. She piled the books on the library tables for them to examine and to read. She arranged a display of the pictures of famous Negroes for them to enjoy and to identify.

That year Martin read all the books on the library table and many more. He knew all the people in the pictures. Miss Lemon had to send him to the main library to get additional books. His favorite poet was Langston Hughes. He enjoyed entertaining the class by reciting Hughes' poem, "Negro Dancers."

Sometimes the class gave imitation radio shows to dramatize stories in Negro history.

They greatly enjoyed portraying different characters before the group. One radio show was built around the story of Crispus Attucks and the Boston Massacre. Another program was based on the participation of Peter Salem in the Revolutionary War. Still other programs were based on Benjamin Banneker and his wooden clock, Harriet Tubman and the Underground Railroad, Frederick Douglass, the abolitionist leader, Booker T. Washington, the educator, George Washington Carver, the scientist, and Matt Henson, the explorer.

When the radio broadcasts were on Negro musicians, the pupils pretended they were Marian Anderson, Thomas Bethune (Blind Tom), Harry T. Burleigh, Roland Hayes, and Madame Sisseretta Jones (Black Patti). They enjoyed pretending to be such famous musicians.

One time Langston Hughes came to Oglethorpe School to visit Miss Lemon's class. His book of poems "The Dream Keeper and Other Poems" was on display on the reading table along with other books about Negroes. The children were thrilled and asked him many questions about his life and work. Martin told Mr. Hughes that he liked his poetry, especially, "Negro Dancers." Mr. Hughes picked up his book of poems and turned to the poem, "Negro Dancers." "Would you like to read this poem for us, young man?" he said to Martin.

The children clapped. Martin smiled. Miss Lemon was amused because she knew that Mr. Hughes was in for a treat.

"I know the poem, sir," Martin replied. "Would you like for me to recite it?" He glanced at Miss Lemon and knew from her smiling face that it would be all right for him to recite for Mr. Hughes as he had done many times for the class.

"By all means, young man," said Mr. Hughes.

He moved to one side and let Martin have the center of the front of the room.

Martin took his place before the class and recited:

NEGRO DANCERS

"Me an' ma baby's
Got two mo' ways,
Two mo' ways to do de Charleston!"
  Da, da,
  Da, da, da!
Two mo' ways to do de Charleston!

(He cut a few steps of the Charleston. The class loved it, and smiled as they waited for the rest.)

Soft light on the tables,
Music gay,
Brown-skin steppers
In a cabaret.

White folks, laugh!
White folks, pray!

"Me an' ma baby's
Got two mo' ways,
Two mo' ways to do de Charleston!"

(He cut a few more steps of the Charleston, then stopped and bowed to the class.)

When he had finished, the class clapped and clapped. They liked both his actions and the poem itself. Finally they stopped clapping and looked at their distinguished visitor.

"That was very well done," he said. "I'm so happy all of you like my poems. It is not often that I hear someone else recite my poems and act them out."

He picked another book of his poems and said to the class, "In this book I've included poems which I thought young people such as you would especially like. 'Negro Dancers' is a great favorite with boys and girls. Another favorite, at least with the boys and girls in Cleveland, Ohio, is 'I, Too.'"

He paused, and Miss Lemon spoke, "That is a favorite with us, too, Mr. Hughes. We talk about the meaning each time some student recites it or I read it. Will you read it for us?"

Mr. Hughes was pleased. He usually read a few poems from his book as he travelled about the country, lecturing to young people. Of course, he didn't really need the book, but he picked it up and started to recite.

I, Too

I, too, sing America.

I am the darker brother.
They send me to eat in the kitchen
When company comes,
But I laugh,
And eat well,
And grow strong.

Tomorrow,
I'll sit at the table

When company comes.
Nobody'll dare
Say to me,
"Eat in the kitchen,"
Then.

Besides,
They'll see how beautiful I am
And be ashamed—

I, too, am America.

When he finished reading this serious poem, the class was silent. It expressed hope for boys and girls who were seeking to become great Americans. Later, Martin often used this poem or parts of it in speeches and sermons.

"Tell us something about your life, Mr. Hughes," one of the girls in the class said.

"Please do," the class chorused.

Mr. Hughes was pleased. "I was born in a small town in Missouri, called Joplin," he began. "I was educated, however, in the public schools of Lawrence, Kansas. Then I went to Central High School in Cleveland, Ohio. I wrote my first short story when I was in high school."

"When did you finish high school?" one of the boys asked.

"A long time ago, in 1920," replied Mr. Hughes, waiting for other questions.

"Did you go to college?" Martin asked.

"Yes, but I didn't stay in college very long," replied Mr. Hughes. "I attended Lincoln University, which is in Pennsylvania, and Columbia University which is in New York. I left college to travel around the world."

"How exciting!" said Martin.

"Yes, it was, young man. I observed people and many cultures and customs. I collected material and did a lot of writing."

"We are traveling around the world right now, Mr. Hughes," said one of the girls.

Mr. Hughes looked puzzled. Then Miss

Lemon explained that the pupils in the social studies class were taking imaginary trips to various countries around the world. "We are leaving Egypt now and are on our way to the Belgian Congo," she said.

Mr. Hughes showed that he understood, and said, "What an interesting way to learn. I learned quite a bit as I made trips to Africa and to Europe by way of the West Coast of the United States, China, and Siberia. As I traveled hundreds of miles far into African jungles and visited with the tribal people, I began to appreciate our ancestors who were brought here. I didn't have much money, so I 'roughed it' in many European countries."

"What does 'roughed it' mean," asked Martin, somewhat perplexed.

Mr. Hughes smiled before he answered him. "'Roughed it' means that I traveled and lived without ordinary everyday comforts and conveniences. I had a tough time, but everything was worth while. I brought back many notes based on my experiences in different countries."

The children remembered Langston Hughes' visit and talked about it for many weeks and months. Their Negro history lessons meant more when they had an opportunity to meet important Negroes like Hughes. Fortunately at Oglethorpe School there were frequent opportunities.

Enjoyment of Negro History

MISS LEMON constantly found ways to enrich her pupils' lives. She made arrangements for displays, exhibits, programs, and presentations of Negro literature and culture in her room. She taught her pupils that they were members of an important American group, and that they were "somebody." She felt they should live and grow in an uplifting environment.

The Negro children at Oglethorpe School seldom saw white persons except those who ran stores and other businesses in the neighborhoods where they lived. They knew that there were white teachers, but most of them taught in the white public schools. There were student or practice teachers at the Oglethorpe School, but all of them were Negroes. Later they would become teachers in Negro public schools.

In order to stimulate her pupils' interest in Negro business activities, Miss Lemon took them on many trips to Negro places of business. She took them to the Negro newspaper, the *Atlanta Daily World*, and introduced them to the owners. She took them to Citizens Trust Company, a Negro bank, and the Atlanta Life Insurance Company, a Negro company. She took them to visit Negro doctors and lawyers, and to hear prominent Negroes speak on topics of special interest to Negroes.

The pupils in Miss Lemon's room always started the day by singing, "Lift Every Voice and Sing." They not only sang the words but they carefully studied the meaning of the words. "Always remember that James Weldon Johnson wrote this song," Miss Lemon reminded them. "Now let us recall who this famous person was."

Then a pupil would answer that James Weldon Johnson was a teacher, a writer, a diplomat, and for many years executive secretary of the National Association for the Advancement of Colored People (NAACP). Other pupils would identify his photograph from among the many photographs on display around the room.

One day Miss Lemon asked, "Does anyone have any other material to share with us on Mr. Johnson?" She looked about for someone to respond. Finally a little girl held up her hand and Miss Lemon said, "Yes, Hattie?"

"I would like to tell how Mr. Johnson came to write the song," she answered.

Hattie had a beautiful soprano voice. It was easy to understand why she would be interested in stories about musicians and music. "I haven't found out much," she said, "but I thought the class might be interested in a few things I have discovered."

"Yes, tell us," said Miss Lemon.

Hattie went before the class and began: "James Weldon Johnson lived in Florida. He had a brother named J. Rosamond Johnson, who sometimes worked with him in writing songs. One would write the words and the other would write the music. James Weldon Johnson often traveled about to speak to groups of adults and children. One day he was to give a speech in Jacksonville, Florida, with many school children present. Accordingly he decided to try to give Negroes hope for the future and help them to realize that they had come a long way."

Miss Lemon interrupted. "Let us check the meaning of your words, 'come a long way,' " she said. "Thomas, what do these words mean?"

"I think they mean that Negroes have helped a lot in building this country," replied Thomas.

"They have done and are doing many important things, even though they have been free from slavery only a short time."

Miss Lemon smiled. She was so proud when a pupil showed that he remembered Negro history. "You explained the meaning well, Thomas," she said. "Now, Hattie, you may continue with your report."

Again Hattie went on speaking to the class. "Mr. Johnson thought it would be nice to give the children a song to sing, so he wrote the words of the song and his brother wrote the music. Five hundred copies of the song were made on a mimeograph machine so that each child could have a copy.

"The day came when Mr. Johnson made his speech. The teachers and the children sang the song, and loved it. Later many of the children who sang the song became teachers, and used their copies to make other copies for their pupils.

Thus all over the country school children and church groups began to sing the song."

Once more Miss Lemon interrupted. "Are Negroes the only persons who like the song?"

"No, white persons like the song, too," replied Hattie. "Sometimes when Mr. Johnson made speeches, the audience would sing the song for him. Sometimes he spoke in places where there were no Negroes present. Then the white children would sing the song. Finally the NAACP adopted it as the Negro National Anthem."

Hattie stopped and looked at Miss Lemon. "That is all of my report," she said.

Miss Lemon was highly pleased. "Very good, Hattie," she said. "Where did you learn the things you just reported to us?"

Hattie went to the library table where books by and about Negroes were displayed and picked up a book. Then she went back to the front of the room and said, "I obtained my information from this autobiography of James Weldon Johnson called *Along This Way.*"

"What is an autobiography?" Miss Lemon asked the class.

A girl named Lucia and Martin held up their hands. Miss Lemon called on Lucia because she wanted to encourage the girl. "An autobiography is the story of a person's life written by himself," replied Lucia.

"Very good," said Miss Lemon. "Do we have many other autobiographies of Negroes on our library table?"

"Yes, we have two others," replied Lucia, "one by Booker T. Washington and one by Frederick Douglass."

"Thank you, Lucia," said Miss Lemon. "Now let us sing the Negro National Anthem."

All the children stood up and sang:

Lift ev'ry voice and sing
'Till earth and heaven ring,

Ring with the harmonies of liberty;
Let our rejoicing rise
High as the list'ning skies,
Let it resound loud as the rolling sea.
Sing a song full of the faith that the dark
   past has taught us;
Sing a song full of the hope that the present
   has brought us;
Facing the rising sun of our new day begun,
Let us march on 'till victory is won.

Stony the road we trod,
Bitter the chastening rod,
Felt in the days when hope unborn had died:
Yet with a steady beat.
Have not our weary feet,
Come to the place for which our fathers
   sighed?
We have come over a way that with tears has
   been watered.
We have come, treading our path thro' the
   blood of the slaughtered
Out of the gloomy past
'Til now we stand at last

Where the white gleam of the bright star is
        cast.

God of our weary years,
God of our silent tears,
Thou who hast brought us thus far on our way,
Thou who hast by Thy might
Let us into the light,
Keep us forever in the path, we pray;
Lest our feet stray from the places, our God
        where we met Thee,
Lest, our hearts drunk with the wine of the
        world, we forget Thee.
Shadowed beneath Thy hand,
May we forever stand,
True to our God,
True to our native land.

As Miss Lemon listened to the children sing the song, she had difficulty fighting back the tears. She realized that they were too young to know what the words really meant, or to understand the depressing conditions which led Mr. Johnson to compose the song. She decided to read to the children from the autobiography. Accordingly she read how Johnson felt that nothing he had ever done had paid him back so fully in satisfaction as being the part creator of the song. He was always thrilled when he heard it sung by Negro children.

Miss Lemon closed the book and looked at the children, who had been listening closely. She was pleased to see that they enjoyed learning about James Weldon Johnson and other famous Negroes. "Have any of you ever seen Mr. Johnson in person?" she asked the class.

Many hands went up, and Miss Lemon called on Thomas. "Yes," he said. "We met Mr. Johnson and heard him speak when he came to Atlanta University for Charter Day last year."

"Good," said Miss Lemon. "Has Mr. Johnson ever had any other important connection with Atlanta University?"

Once again many hands went up, and this time

Miss Lemon called on Martin. "Mr. Johnson was a graduate of Atlanta University in 1894, when the school was not very old," said Martin. "I've done a lot of reading about Atlanta schools. Someday I should like to give a report on some of the schools here."

"Certainly, Martin," said Miss Lemon. "You may give your report next Thursday. We'll enjoy hearing it."

A pupil asked Miss Lemon whether she would read a selection from "God's Trombones," a book of Negro sermons by James Weldon Johnson. Martin brought a copy of the book from the library table, and she sat down in front of the class. The pupils gathered around her to listen.

Miss Lemon turned to a poem, "The Creation." It was one of her favorites that she often read with the class.

In order to bring out the full effect of the poem, it was necessary to have different voices represent different speakers. Sometimes Miss Lemon would let the children read the parts, and at other times she would read the poem alone and change her voice to represent different persons. Today she decided to read the whole poem by herself, using intonation or changes in her voice to represent different persons. The children's eyes never left her face.

And God stepped out on space,
And He looked around and said,
"I'm lonely—
I'll make me a world."

When Thursday came, Martin brought his material to school for his report. He had gathered the information from books in his own library at home. Ever since he had been quite young he had had a paper route, delivering the *Atlanta Journal* each evening. He used some of the money that he earned to buy books.

Martin was interested in education, and when he was reading about different Negroes he read about the history of Negro schools. Some of the books which he read explained that Negroes had not always had a chance to go to school and learn. He found out that even Atlanta Negroes had not always had schools which they could attend.

One day he happened to find interesting information about the Younge Street School, which he had attended, and also about the Oglethorpe School. He took notes and decided that he would like to give a report on the schools to his class. Now the opportunity had come and he was ready to proceed.

Miss Lemon told him to come before the class and take a seat to read his report. She could see that it was somewhat long, but she felt that the pupils would be interested. Martin held his paper before him and started to read:

The first school I attended was called the Younge Street School. It was named after the street where it is located. The land for building this school was donated by a Negro Bishop whose name was Henry McNeal Turner. A Bishop is more important than a preacher and has more power. He is in charge of preachers. Bishop Turner was in the African Methodist Church.

Several years passed before a school was built, because many people thought Negroes didn't need to go to school. Negroes paid taxes and a part of the taxes was spent for running schools. Still there were no public schools for Negroes.

After Bishop Turner donated the land for a public school, the Negroes asked the board of education to put up the building. Finally, in 1911, the first modern brick school for Negroes was built in Atlanta. The teachers and the first principal came from colleges here in Georgia.

This one school could not serve all the Negroes who wanted to learn, so in 1915, a few Negroes were allowed to attend evening classes. Some were able to work during the day and go to school at night. This is how my father got his high school education.

Years before Bishop Turner had been elected to the Georgia Legislature, but he was not permitted to take his seat. No Negroes were allowed to be in the legislatures at that time. Bishop Turner rebelled at the idea, but nobody in authority would listen to him. Later, however, he was elected again and permitted to take his seat.

Bishop Turner was an outstanding leader. President Ulysses S. Grant made him postmaster of Georgia, and afterwards he became a government detective. He died in 1915, just a few years after he donated the land for the Younge Street School.

Next I attended the Howard School in Atlanta. This school was built in 1922 to replace an old dilapidated building that was built many years before. It was named for David T. Howard, the first Negro embalmer registered in Georgia. He had the first funeral home in the Negro area of Atlanta. He was important because he donated money to educate young people. All he ever asked of them was that they become a credit to the race. He was one of the founders and one of the officers of the first Negro bank in Atlanta, and he was a leader in church.

At this point Martin paused, wondering whether he should go on reading. He looked at Miss Lemon, and said, "This report is long. Shall I go on now, or wait till another day?"

"Go on," said the pupils. "We want to learn what you found out about Oglethorpe School."

Martin went on reading:

Oglethorpe School was started as a practice school for Atlanta University. It was named for General James Oglethorpe, the founder of the colony of Georgia. Georgia was a colony before it was a state.

In 1867, two years after the end of the War between the States, twelve men came down from the North to start schools for Negroes. One of these twelve men was a minister named Edmund Asa Ware, who was the real founder of Atlanta University.

Mr. Ware held his first school for Negroes in an old freight car. One of his greatest problems was to find qualified teachers. The Negroes had just been freed and one knew only about as much as another. Mr. Ware started in on this problem at once and began to train teachers.

At first Atlanta University was a primary school, a grammar school, a high school, and a college combined. Friends of Mr. Ware came from the North to help him. After years of hard work, they purchased land for the first school building.

This first building had a dormitory upstairs for the boys and girls and their teachers. The lower floor was used for instruction. All the classes were held there.

The school grew rapidly because Negroes were eager to secure an education and there was no other school to attend in Atlanta. More teachers were needed and many came from the best Northern Schools. They came from Harvard, Yale, Dartmouth, Chicago,

Wellesley, Mount Holyoke, and Boston. All came because they had a great interest in Negroes and wanted to help them succeed.

Today Atlanta University is one of the oldest schools in the South devoted to higher education for Negroes. The first class from the university was graduated in 1876. The school has been growing and serving Negroes ever since.

Mr. Ware realized that the university needed a school where students could observe teaching and practice teaching. In 1904 he opened Oglethorpe School for these purposes. Children could start to school here in the kindergarten and go all the way through college. I never went to kindergarten myself, but did my first work at the Younge Street School, which I told you about.

The class enjoyed Martin's report and applauded him. He was pleased and put his report on display with other materials about Negroes.

Listening and Thinking

WHEN MARTIN reached his teenage years a few people still called him M. L., but most people called him Martin or Mike. By now he had formed many principles and conclusions which were to guide him throughout life. He was talented and eager to secure better ways of living for people of his race.

For years he had lived in a community where everyone talked about race and racial problems. As a small child, he had seen his father refuse to take insults from white people. In church he had heard his father preach repeatedly against oppression of Negro rights. At school he had been taught to hold his head high and refuse to accept discrimination.

At home and in school he had read stories about Negro leaders of the past and had tried to keep up with current Negro leaders. He had gained respect for people of his race by reading the Negro newspaper, the *Atlanta Daily World*. The owners of the newspaper were friends of his family and he was always welcome there.

He had been impressed with the number of people coming to his father's church. He had observed their responses when his father urged them to improve themselves and he had noted the happiness on their faces when he praised them for their diligent efforts. As he had moved about the church, he had heard one member after another praise his father. One member had said, "Rev. King is a great preacher. We're fortunate to have him."

"Yes," said another. "He doesn't drive us, but

requests us to do the right things. He keeps us working together for our rights."

Martin had taken note of all these things and had remembered with pride that his father's church usually had led Baptist churches in giving to missions and educational causes. His father always had helped persons who couldn't help themselves and had promoted the cause of education.

Martin was proud of his father, and he was proud of his mother, too. By now his mother was playing a brand-new pipe organ which the church had installed. The *Atlanta Daily World* had said that this new organ was one of the best in the city. People were excited about the new organ and they flocked to the church to listen.

Once Martin's father preached a sermon on "The Kind of House We Build." The sermon made him think more about what he wanted to become in life. He knew that he wanted to be somebody important like his father. He wanted to become a good speaker so that people would listen to him. He wanted to be able to help people live better lives.

This year his father was chairman of the Atlanta Citizens' Committee, which was trying to get equal salaries for Negro teachers. He was also chairman of the men's division of the Fulton County Civilian Defense Council, which was training persons to protect themselves in case of air raids during World War II. Also he was working to help Negroes secure jobs to help out during the war years.

From the pulpit on Sunday, Rev. King told his members to register at various schools for civilian jobs. Hundreds of people registered for jobs to help out in the war effort while our armed forces were fighting abroad. Many Negroes were members of the armed forces fighting along with whites for their country.

Nearly every Sunday Martin listened to two sermons, one by his father at the Ebenezer Baptist Church and the other by Rev. William Holmes Borders at the Wheat Street Baptist Church. These two churches were on corners only one block apart. Usually on Sunday, Martin would go to Wheat Street Baptist Church and sit in the balcony to listen to Rev. Borders. Then he would return to the Ebenezer Baptist Church to hear his father preach. He idolized both preachers and liked to compare their sermons.

On one particular Sunday, Rev. Borders preached a sermon on "Dethroning Self" and his father preached a sermon on "Follow Thou Me." Martin listened to both sermons with great interest and thoughtfulness. As he listened, he wondered whether he should study medicine, law, or the ministry. He remembered both sermons for years and often spoke of "dethroning self" and "following God's direction, not man's."

Several weeks later young people packed the Wheat Street Baptist Church for a Negro History Week observance. A senior from the Booker T. Washington High School talked about the contributions Negroes were making during World War II. He told how Negroes were fighting and dying for their country.

The very next morning Martin rode a street

car to school and noticed a sign which he thought was insulting to Negroes. This sign instructed Negroes to fill up the seats from the back to the front. It instructed white persons to fill up the seats from the front to the back.

Later in the day Martin talked with his friend Larry Williams about the sign. Then bitterly he said, "I wonder whether the boys fighting for our country ride all together on trucks to the front lines or whether they are segregated on the trucks."

Larry merely smiled. He was a few years older than Martin. He had seen many examples of segregation about the community and had expressed disgust many times before.

I Am Somebody

MARTIN was influenced by almost everything in the community. He read the local news, observed widely, and thought about all that he read or saw. Many persons in the community, besides his own father and mother, had influence on him. One of these people was Rev. Borders of the Wheat Street Baptist Church.

For many years the Wheat Street Baptist Church had had a small membership. It had had only a few members late in the 1930's, when Rev. Borders had come there to preach. Martin's father had been pastor of Ebenezer Baptist Church nearly ten years before.

By the time Martin was growing up, Rev. Borders had built up a strong church and was well known about the city. He worked in the heart of the slums, which were only a few blocks from his church. He went into bars and poolrooms and invited people to come to his church. He even invited them to come in old clothes.

As he visited these places, he often told stories from the Bible. The men stared at him, but they listened. He seemed to understand them. At first some of the members of his church questioned what he was doing, but they changed their minds as people began to flock to his church.

Sunday after Sunday as he stood up to preach he would start off as follows:

"You have been told often by many authorities that you are no good, and I can see by your faces that some of you believe you are no good. Well, I'm here to tell you that you are wrong.

You are somebody. Let me tell you of the great heritage of your ancestors."

Following this introduction, he would tell them about Negroes who had been famous in the history of our country. All the while Martin would sit in his favorite balcony seat and listen and think.

One Sunday morning Martin was especially interested when he heard Rev. Borders say, "A preacher must always be the leader of his people. He must go where the people are and invite them in. He must tell them that Jesus loves them, and that there is room enough in heaven for us all. Just as Moses led the children of Israel through the wilderness, the Negro preacher of today must lead people hopefully toward a better life tomorrow."

Martin thought that the ideas behind these words were beautiful and the words themselves were beautiful. The words were well chosen and simple enough for the audience to understand. They were the kind of words that made the Bible come alive.

One other Sunday morning Martin was fascinated when he heard Rev. Borders tell his people, "You're the finest people in the world, I love you. I love every one of you."

By now Martin had great respect for preachers like his father and Rev. Borders. Now and then he would stand on a street corner with friends, and practice speaking like Rev. Borders. He also would imitate his father, because he realized that both men were powerful speakers.

Rev. Borders sometimes spoke from the top of his church through a loud speaker. Occasionally he would use the chimes of the church for background. Every Saturday he recited his famous speech "I Am Somebody." Nearly always Martin and his friends gathered before the church with a large throng of people to hear him.

I Am Somebody

I am Somebody—
    I am a poet in Langston Hughes.
    I am a creator of rhyme in
        Paul Lawrence Dunbar.
    I am a Christian statesman in
        J. P. E. Lee.
    I am a diplomat in Fred Douglass.
I am Somebody—
I am Somebody—
    I am a soldier in Colonel Young.
    I am courage in Crispus Attucks.
    I am a humorist in Bert Williams.
    I am a radio artist in Dorothy Maynor.
    I am a world famous tenor in
        Roland Hayes.
    I am a baritone in Paul Robeson.
I am Somebody—
I am Somebody—
    I am an athlete in Bennie Jefferson.
    I am a sprinter in Ralph Metcalfe.
    I am an intelligent pen in the hand of
        DuBois.

I am a college president in John Hope.
I am a fighter in
    Samuel Howard Archer.
I am a breaker of world records in
    Jesse Owens.
I am Somebody—
I am Somebody—
    I am an orator in P. James Bryant.
    I am a preacher in C. T. Walker and
        L. K. Williams.
    I am a composer in R. Nathaniel Dett.
    I am an actor in Richard B. Harrison.
    I am a boxer in Armstrong Williams.
    I am a knock-out punch in Joe Louis.
I am Somebody—
I am Somebody—
    I am a scientist in
        George Washington Carver.
    I am an industrial educator in
        Booker T. Washington.
    I am a congressman in Oscar DePriest
    and Arthur Mitchell.
    I am a skin specialist in Lawless and
    teach what I know at

Northwestern.

I am a pathologist in Julian Lewis and
serve on the University of Chicago
faculty.

I am the first successful operator on
the human heart in
Daniel Hale Williams.

I am Somebody—
I am Somebody—

I am a marksman in Dorie Miller.

I am a register of the treasury in
Judson Lyons.

I am loyalty in the Armed Services.

I am insight in Sojourner Truth.

I am an advocator of Justice in
Walter White.

I am a leader in A. Phillip Randolph.

I am Somebody—
I am Somebody—

I am a moulder of character in
Nannie Burroughs.

I am a banker in R. R. Wright and
L. D. Milton.

I am a certified Public Accountant in

Jesse Blayton.
I am a sculptor in Henry O. Tanner.
I am a businessman in
    Alonzo Herndon.
I am a grand specimen of womanhood
    in Mary McLeod Bethune.
I am Somebody—
I am Somebody—
    I am an insurance executive in
        C. C. Spaulding.
    I am a biologist in Just of Howard.
    I am a Historian in Carter Woodson.
    I am a lover of education in
        Charlotte Hawkins Brown.
    I am a beautician in Mesdames
        Walker, Washington and Malone.
    I am a trustee in slavery —I protected
        my Master's wives and daughters
        while he fought to keep the chains
        of slavery about my body.
I am Somebody—
I am Somebody—
    I am a Bishop in W. A. Fountain.
    I am a Ball of Fire in Richard Allen.
    I am a laborer in John Henry.

122

> I am a Christian in "Tom," for indeed,
> I practiced the religion of Jesus at
> points better than my master from
> whom I learned it.

I am Somebody—

Long after Rev. Borders finished speaking, Martin and his friends would linger on to talk about the speech. He and his friends often discussed Rev. Borders' sermons to see whether they had derived the same meanings and understandings. Sometimes Rev. Borders would come and join them because he wanted them to become strong spiritual leaders.

Learning to Think and to Act

When Martin was ready for high school, he entered the Booker T. Washington High School in Atlanta. He entered the school early for his age, because he had been permitted to take examinations and skip some of the subjects.

One of his favorite teachers at the Booker T. Washington High School was Miss Grace Bradley. She took a special interest in him and encouraged him to enter the Elks Oratorical Contest. An oratorical contest is a contest of speaking ability.

The Elks contest was open to high school pupils all over the country. There was a separate contest in each state. Each speaker was to choose a subject from a list published by the Elks Club. Each subject had something to do with the Constitution. Martin chose the subject, "The Negro and the Constitution."

Miss Bradley helped him collect material for his speech. She helped him organize the ideas and checked all the words which he used. She listened as he practiced giving the speech.

The contest in Georgia was held at Dublin, which was a long bus ride from Atlanta. Miss Bradley went with Martin to give him encouragement. Martin gave a brilliant speech, but he did not win the contest. He was disappointed, but the contest had been fun.

After the contest Miss Bradley and Martin boarded a bus to return to Atlanta. They found a seat in front of Negroes who sat in seats at the back of the bus. The driver was supposed to fill the bus from front to back with white people.

Then, if more white persons got on than there were seats in front, the Negroes sitting near the front of their section were supposed to get up and let the white persons sit down.

The bus stopped along the way to let many white people on. Soon the front of the bus filled up and two white people had to stand up. Miss Bradley and Martin were sitting in the seats the Negroes were supposed to give up, but they were talking and didn't notice the two white persons standing.

The white people in the bus looked at them furiously. Finally the bus driver stopped the bus and ordered Miss Bradley and Martin to surrender their seats. "Get up and give up your seats," he said.

Martin looked at Miss Bradley. They hesitated and the bus driver walked back to them and started cursing. Miss Bradley got up, looked at Martin and said, "It's the law."

Martin never forgot this experience. He told about it many times and how it helped him to realize the many insults Negroes suffered every day. "I decided right then that someday I would do something about those daily pinpricks and insults," he said.

Several months later Miss Bradley had another experience which infuriated Martin. She and her sister were starting from Atlanta on a bus to Athens, Georgia. Her sister entered the bus first, gave her ticket to the driver, and took a seat in the rear. Next Miss Bradley stepped on the bus and started to hand her ticket to the driver, but he refused to take it. "No niggers are allowed on this bus," he said.

"My sister is already on the bus," Miss Bradley explained, but the driver chose to ignore her. Then she went to one of the windows, and told her sister to get off.

The sister got off and the two women tried to

board other busses but were turned down. They protested this discrimination, were accused of disorderly conduct and were arrested. Finally they were taken into court.

All this puzzled Martin. He asked Miss Bradley why she protested when she wouldn't let him protest on the bus coming from Dublin. She explained by saying, "At that time I was responsible for you. When you are responsible for someone else, you think of the other person, not of yourself. I was obligated to see that you returned home safely. If I had protested, or allowed you to do so, we both might have been hurt. I had to think. Had I been alone, I might have protested."

Martin noticed that she used the word *think*. Already he had learned, both from his father and Rev. Borders, that a leader must think. Then he decided that he would always think first and then act. Thinking must precede acting.

Mountain-Top Experiences

MARTIN loved sports, though he never played on any school teams. Often he stopped to watch children play at the Howard School playground, which was near his home. Sometimes he threw balls to the children, and caught balls, which they threw back to him. Most of them knew him as the son of the preacher at the big church on the corner.

As a growing young man, Martin's favorite exercises were walking, playing tennis, and swimming. He could play table tennis well, and he could play a good game of pool, but he never hung around pool halls to play.

Occasionally, when he could tear himself away from reading, he took part in baseball games. He was both a good pitcher and a good batter. Whenever he hit the ball, he would take off for first base with great speed. He was an excellent runner and could steal a base before the opposing players could bat an eyelash. Often after he had outsmarted them by stealing a base, he would stand and shake all over with laughter. He was full of fun, and the boys liked to have him around.

As he grew into his teens, he could handle himself well in a fight. Every now and then he would challenge a friend to "take him to the grass" to settle an argument, but fighting was not his way of settling differences. Everyone knew, however, that he was no coward.

Martin was never shy about disagreeing. He would continually argue for what he thought was right, but always he was a good sport.

Whenever possible, he resorted to talking his way out rather than fighting his way out.

Even though Martin never took active part in sports, he enjoyed watching teams play. He took particular interest in watching his brother A. D. and his friend Willie play football with the Howard Junior High School Ramblers.

At the end of one season, the team ended up in debt. Then a Stunt and Talent Night was held to help pay off the debt. In these performances, youngsters were asked to demonstrate their talents. The first talent night was so successful, that the contest became an annual affair. The money which was raised made it possible to establish football at the Howard Junior High School as part of the school program.

About this time Martin's father was in the middle of a drive to clean up Auburn Avenue. This drive was part of a crusade against vice and crime in all the dives up and down the

street. One of the dives was a notorious wine shop, where many unfortunate persons loitered and wasted their time. Everyone knew that much of the trouble was caused by the wine shop and its patrons.

In leading the fight Rev. King was supported by other ministers, organized Negro leaders, business and professional men, and interested citizens. When the committee members went before the city council to state their case, the lawyer for the wine shop declared that this was a case of Negroes against a white merchant. Rev. King explained that this was not so. He pointed out that one of the best regulated and most orderly places in the whole neighborhood was conducted by white persons.

From such experiences as this Martin learned that the fight was against injustice and crime in the community and not against white people. He learned that not all white people were wrong, but that many wrong-doers also were Negroes. According to his father's point of view, anybody who kept vice and crime going was considered wrong. The crusade was against crime in the community, not gainst Negroes or whites. The committee sought to clean up Auburn Avenue, and eventually did.

Another important fight this year was conducted by the Citizens Committee on Public Education. This committee pointed out that public education for Negroes was far below standard. Only three years before Negro children had attended school only three and one-half hours a day.

By now conditions were a little better, but Negro education still was below standard. Far less money was spent to educate a Negro child than to educate a white child. In the city of Atlanta, there was only one public school for every 2040 Negro children whereas there was one school for every 855 white children. The committee members considered this ratio unfair.

Martin's father was in the thick of both these fights. He wanted to help remove slum businesses from his area. He wanted Negro children to have an equal chance with white children to obtain an education. He was always ready to support causes for the betterment of people.

At home Martin heard many discussions of community problems. On Sunday he heard his father present some of the problems to his congregation. Always his father urged the members to work together to obtain better lives for themselves and their children.

Although his father's sermons were spirited, Martin always found great peace in his father's preaching. This year his father preached a sermon, called "Mountain-Top Experiences," which Martin never forgot. Later on Rev. Borders preached a series of sermons on the same subject. Martin listened to all these sermons with great interest.

The general theme of the sermons covered the experiences of the children of Israel being delivered out of Egypt. The climax came when Moses went to the mountain-top where he met his God.

Years later, just before Martin's life was snuffed out by an assassin, he preached that he felt he had "been to the mountain-top."

Building for the Future

WHEN Martin was fifteen years of age, he entered Morehouse College, a men's college noted for its excellent training. The freshman class that year included one hundred seventy young men. In his opening remarks to the class, the president, Dr. Benjamin Mays, talked about the importance of scholarship and character. The college courses continuously pointed up striving for finer manhood in everyday living and taking places of service in the community.

When Martin entered Morehouse College, he was still undecided about his career for life. He was uncertain whether he wanted to become a physician or a lawyer, or a preacher. Often he discussed careers with his friends, Walter McCall and Larry Williams.

Walter McCall planned to become a lawyer. When Martin talked with Walter, he thought he might become a lawyer and Walter's partner. Larry Williams, on the other hand, planned to become a minister. When Martin talked with Larry, he thought he might become a minister and work with Larry.

After two years at Morehouse College, Martin finally decided that he wanted to become a minister. Both his father and mother were highly pleased with his decision. His father arranged for him to preach a trial sermon in the Ebenezer Baptist Church. The members liked his preaching and in 1947 he became assistant pastor of his father's church.

The next year, he graduated from Morehouse College with a bachelor of arts degree. He was

only nineteen years of age, but he was sure of himself. More than that, he was ambitious, eager to become an outstanding minister.

In the fall of 1948, Martin entered Crozer Theological Seminary in Chester, Pennsylvania. He was determined to prepare himself well for his chosen career. Accordingly, he must secure as much training as possible.

At Crozer, Martin was one of six Negro students in a total enrollment of one hundred students. This was his first real experience in competing with whites, but he made a good record. His years of reading and studying provided a good foundation for his training.

Martin worked hard to show that he was just like any other student. All the while he knew he was on trial with the white students, but he tried not be guilty of things whites often said about Negroes. Often they said that Negroes were lazy, undependable, and inferior. They also said that Negroes wanted to be granted special rights and privileges.

Through the years Martin won the respect of the students and was elected president of the senior class. When he graduated in 1951, he was granted an award as the most outstanding student in the class. He also received a fellowship of $1200 for further study.

Martin used his fellowship to attend Boston University where he worked for his Ph.D. degree. While he was a student here, he met Coretta Scott, a student at the Boston New England Conservatory of Music. The two of them soon fell in love and were married in 1953, at her parents' home in Alabama.

When Martin Luther King graduated in 1954, he had offers of several jobs, some to teach and one to become dean of a college. He discussed the situation with his wife and together they decided to return to the South where he could continue in the ministry. In the spring he became pastor at the Dexter Avenue Baptist Church of Montgomery, Alabama.

A few months later, the Supreme Court ruled that there could be no more segregation in public schools. This important decision was destined to have great effect on the life of Martin Luther King, Jr. from then on.

Revolt against Bus Segregation

THE REV. MARTIN Luther King, Jr., was busy at first becoming acquainted with the members of his congregation at the Dexter Avenue Baptist Church. This was a large church and he felt that he should come to know all the members well. The members liked him and he soon was off to a good start.

It was not long before young Rev. King began to take an interest in Negro problems in the city of Montgomery. There were about 50,000 Negroes and about 70,000 white people in the city. Nearly one half of the Negro men were employed in the lowest types of jobs. About half of the Negro women who worked were servants in the homes of white people.

There were two separate communities in Montgomery. One was for the white people, and the other was for the Negroes. Negroes and white people used the same shopping centers, but Negroes usually had to wait while white people were served. The schools were segregated, with Negro children going to certain schools and white children to other schools. Negroes and whites rode buses together, but the white people rode in the section toward the front and the Negroes in the section toward the back. There was no organization in the city through which Negroes and whites could meet and work out their problems together.

There was a chapter of the National Association for the Advancement of Colored People (NAACP) in Montgomery. This chapter was very busy handling the many Negro problems of the city. The new Rev. King's church was active in the NAACP drive to get people registered to vote. Only 2,000 of the 50,000 Negroes in Montgomery were registered. Dexter Avenue Baptist Church led all the other churches in the city in this important drive.

Rev. King became more and more interested in the NAACP. Within a year he was elected to the executive committee of the organization. As he attended the monthly meetings, he began to see more clearly the many racial problems bothering the community.

At about the same time Rev. King began working with the NAACP, he joined the new Alabama Council on Human Rights. This organization held its regular business meetings in a conference room of his church. A few months after he joined the Council, he was elected Vice-President. The Council was composed mostly of Negro ministers, but it also included two white ministers who were very active in the fight against segregation.

The city buses were more or less uncomfortable for both Negroes and whites to ride. The Negroes were made to pay their fares at the front door, then get off and reboard the buses at the rear. After taking their money, many times the drivers would drive off without allowing them time to get on at the rear. Many times the drivers would call the Negroes "niggers," "black cows," or "black apes." In many cases after they entered buses they were forced to stand by empty seats reserved for whites, even though no white people were using them.

Perhaps the worst part of segregation on the buses was the practice of making Negroes seated in the Negro section get up and give their seats to whites. This frequently happened when buses became filled. Then, if a Negro refused to stand and move back, he would be arrested.

Things came to a head over bus segregation on December 1, 1955. Mrs. Rosa Parks, an attractive Negro seamstress, boarded a bus in downtown Montgomery. This was the same bus she had boarded many times after a hard day's work. Today she was tired and eager to get off her aching feet. Accordingly she sat down in the first seat in the Negro section behind the section that was reserved for white passengers.

At stops along the way the bus soon filled with passengers and a few white people had to stand. Then the bus driver ordered Mrs. Parks and three other Negroes to get up and let the white people have their seats. The other Negroes got up immediately, but Mrs. Parks looked the driver straight in the eye and said, "No."

At first the driver was surprised, wondering whether he had heard correctly. When Mrs. Parks clung to her seat, however, and held her head proudly in the air, he realized that he was facing trouble. Accordingly, he stopped his bus, called the police, and had her arrested. Her arrest attracted wide attention because she was one of the most respected people in the Negro community. It helped to start a Negro revolt not only in Montgomery but all across the nation.

An active fighter for Negro's rights at that time was a man named E. D. Nixon of Montgomery, who was a pullman porter. He also was an official in the Brotherhood of Sleeping Car Porters, an organization that protected the rights of Negro porters. Each day he reported to his train and traveled to a certain town and back again. This round trip was known as his run. Along the way he waited on the passengers, carrying their grips and helping them to travel in comfort.

When Mr. Nixon heard what had happened to Mrs. Parks, he became very angry. He happened to be at home at the time and decided to arrange to get her out on bond. In the meantime word of her arrest spread gradually through the Negro community. This arrest happened too late to be reported in the newspaper, but as people used their telepones to call one another, the news spread throughout the community and everybody became very angry.

Mr. Nixon went down to the jail, put up the necessary bail for Mrs. Parks, then took her home. That night he said to his wife, "Our people should just stop riding the buses."

"Stop dreaming," she said in reply. "Put out the light and go to sleep."

By now Mr. Nixon was too excited to go to sleep. Instead, he took a piece of paper and started to write down the names of people he wished to contact. One of these names was Rev. Martin Luther King, Jr.

Early the next morning, Mr. Nixon called Rev. King and told him what had happened to Mrs.

Parks the night before. Rev. King listened with great interest and said that he was shocked to hear of such a humiliating incident.

Mr. Nixon went on talking with great feeling. "We just can't take this sort of thing any longer," he said. "I have already called Rev. Ralph Abernathy of the First Baptist Church, and he has agreed to help with the idea."

Rev. Abernathy was a close personal friend of Rev. King, and the two of them often worked together on community projects. "What idea do you have in mind?" Rev. King asked.

"To boycott the buses," replied Mr. Nixon. "I feel we have to make these white folks come to see that they can't push us around. They must know that we won't accept this kind of treatment any longer."

Rev. King agreed with Mr. Nixon that to stop riding the buses would be a good way to protest. Then for a while he and Rev. Abernathy and Mr.

Nixon telephoned one another, exchanging ideas about the boycott and making plans on how to carry it out successfully.

Rev. King and Rev. Abernathy got permission from the president of the Baptist Ministerial Alliance to call all the Baptist ministers in the city. The president of this organization agreed that a bus boycott was a good idea. Accordingly all the Baptist ministers of the city were notified.

Fortunately the Negro Methodist ministers were holding a meeting that day. An announcement of the boycott was made at the meeting and the ministers agreed to cooperate. Important civic leaders were notified throughout the Negro community.

The aroused Negroes decided to hold a meeting. Mr. Nixon had to leave the city to work on the railroad. In his absence Rev. L. Roy Bennett, president of the Negro ministers in Montgomery, took charge of the meeting.

Everybody agreed that the time had come to act. Action was taken approving a one-day boycott for Monday, December 5. All Negroes were to stay off the city buses on that day.

The Negro ministers of the city agreed to notify their congregations of the boycott on the following Sunday. Then on Monday evening a mass meeting would be held at the Holt Street Baptist Church to decide whether or not the boycott should be continued.

The meeting was attended by many leaders in the Negro community. Negroes were present from many walks of life. There were ministers, teachers, lawyers, doctors, business men and women, and persons engaged in numerous other occupations. All were meeting to work for freedom from insults and injustices of the past.

Not only in Montgomery, but all across the nation Negroes were tired. They were beginning to realize that what affected one Negro affected all other Negroes. They were beginning to realize that being trained in various professions really meant nothing. Professional and trained Negroes were subjected to the same treatment as Negro bums loitering on the streets or wallowing in the gutter.

Negroes from all walks of life were fast beginning to realize that they needed to work together to stop what had been happening to them for years. They must not only carry on a bus boycott, but they must demand their rights in many other situations. They decided to wage war against segregation as never before.

Over 7,000 leaflets were printed and distributed to the Negro community. The leaflets told the Negroes to stay off the buses on Monday, December 5, and to walk, take a cab, or share a ride. Then the leaflet told them they were to come to a mass meeting on Monday evening for further instructions.

By accident, news of the planned boycott reached the white newspaper and the newspaper carried an article about it. The Negroes looked upon this article as an attempt to frighten them from taking part in the boycott, particularly those who worked in white people's homes. For years many Negroes had depended on working for white folks, cooking for them and cleaning their homes and lawns for pitiful wages. All the while they had been afraid to protest the injustices they had suffered.

The article in the newspaper only served to make the Negroes angry and all the more determined. Negroes who had not received the leaflet read the article in the newspaper. Thus all the Negroes in the city came to know about the boycott and the mass meeting at the Holt Street Baptist Church. When Monday evening came Negroes filled the church to overflowing to receive further instructions. The church was packed inside and thousands stood about outside to listen through loud speakers.

Later, the whites demanded that the loud speakers be cut off because they were causing a disturbance. But the thousands of Negroes outside the church stood quietly listening, eager to be counted in on the movement which was to start a Negro revolution.

When Rev. King reached the Holt Street Baptist Church, he had to park four blocks away. He had to work his way through thousands of persons outside the church. Then, after he entered the church, it took him fifteen minutes to make his way up front to the other leaders.

This evening Rev. King was supposed to tell the listening throngs what had happened. He had been too busy during the day to prepare a speech. All he had time to do was to outline what he wanted to say.

The 7,000 leaflets had been printed at Rev.

King's church on the mimeograph machine. That morning he and his wife had risen early to observe buses on the day of the boycott. The first bus had passed their house at 6:00 a. m. and they had looked out to see whether or not Negroes were riding. The bus was empty, and all day the buses were empty.

By 9:30 that morning, Rev. King had been at his church directing committees to do all sorts of things. Many women and young people had come to distribute leaflets or to make calls or to do whatever he felt was necessary.

During the afternoon the leaders in the boycott movement had met and formed a new organization, called the Montgomery Improvement Association (MIA). Rev. King was elected its first president. This association was to play an important part in community affairs later.

Rev. King spoke calmly but firmly at the meeting. He explained that Mrs. Parks had been tried early that morning for disobeying the city segregation ordinance or law. She had been found guilty and fined. This was the first time a Negro had ever been found guilty of disobeying the segregation law. In the past when Negroes had been arrested, they either had been charged with disorderly conduct or their cases had been dismissed.

Rev. King's speech was an overwhelming success. All the listening he had done in his father's church and all the reading he had done came out in what he said. He ended his speech by explaining the Negro's right to protest. The members of the vast audience listened to every word. They were ready to move and enthusiastically let it be known.

This was Martin Luther King's first real act of leadership in the fight for human rights. One old lady in the crowd remarked, "I've been here a long time. I've been through insults a long,

long time. I've seen leaders start leading us out of this mess, but this time I know we'll never turn back. This is the greatest Negro leader I've seen in all my old lifetime."

Later as the bus boycott continued, this old lady walked four miles daily to work. One day she was asked whether her feet were tired. She smiled broadly and replied with spirit, "My feet is tired, but my soul is rested." This idea became a Montgomery Freedom song.

Mrs. Parks was introduced at the meeting and received a standing ovation from the crowd. She was their symbol of courage and hope. She had been unafraid to stand up for her rights. Now all those present at the meeting were ready to stand up for their rights, too.

Rev. Abernathy read what the boycott was hoping to gain. The group decided it wanted:

(1) courteous treatment on the part of the bus drivers.

(2) passengers to be seated on a first-come, first-served basis with Negroes seated from the back toward the front in a bus and whites seated from the front toward the back.

(3) Negro drivers for buses where most of the passengers were Negroes.

A motion was made that these three points be included in the protest. Everyone in the audience stood in favor of the motion. Persons who were already standing raised their hands in agreement. The people both inside and outside the church cheered at the result of the vote. Their cheers showed their determination to back this first important movement to fight segregation in the community.

The Negro Revolt was on. All the while, Rev. King and Rev. Abernathy worked closely together. One other person who was of great assistance to Rev. King was his wife, Coretta. He knew that he could always count on Rev. Abernathy and Coretta for wise counsel and advice.

The bus boycott lasted more than a few days, more than a few weeks, and more than a few months. It lasted for over a year. In February the police arrested over 100 Negroes, including Mrs. Parks and Rev. King.

Later Thurgood Marshall, the chief attorney for the NAACP, went to Montgomery for a conference with Negro leaders regarding the bus boycott. They decided to take the problem of the segregated city buses into the courts. In taking this action, they had to prove that Negroes were paying the same fares as white persons, but not getting equal treatment.

In June the Federal Court ruled that separate seating on city buses was against the law. The city of Montgomery and the bus company, who were the defendents, carried the case to the United States Supreme Court, the highest court in the land. In December the Supreme Court ruled that bus segregation was against the law, not only in Montgomery but everywhere else in the United States.

Finally when the buses were desegregated in Montgomery, the three Negro leaders, Rev. King, Rev. Abernathy, and Mr. Nixon rode the first desegregated bus in the city. The desegregation decision left many hard feelings among white people. Mrs. Parks, who had been the first person arrested, spent two years trying to find a place to work. Finally she had to leave Montgomery and move elsewhere.

As the Negroes started to ride the buses, they had to take many insults and suffer many grievances, but they did not fight back with violence. They did not fight back with bombs, guns, or other ways of hurting or killing people. Rev. King had explained to them the importance of nonviolence.

In Search
of Peace

In 1957, about one year after the bus boycott and desegregation in Montgomery, sixty prominent Negro leaders met at the Ebenezer Baptist Church in Atlanta. These leaders, most of whom were ministers, came from ten southern states. One of those who came was Rev. Fred Shuttlesworth from Birmingham. The leaders decided to form a new organization, the Southern Christian Leadership Conference.

One of the leaders in this movement was Rev. Martin Luther King, Jr. He urged all the leaders to fight for human dignity for Negroes, but to achieve liberties through nonviolent activities.

He was elected the first president of the organization, and the headquarters were located in Atlanta, not far from the Ebenezer Baptist Church. Rev. Shuttlesworth was elected secretary of the new organization.

Some time later, Rev. King decided to resign as pastor of the Dexter Avenue Baptist Church in Montgomery. He decided to move back to Atlanta to join his father at the Ebenezer Baptist Church. His father was pastor of the church, and he became co-pastor. Rev. Abernathy also left Montgomery and moved to Atlanta, where he became pastor of the Hunter Street Baptist Church. Both men felt that they would have greater opportunities to fight for freedom in Atlanta, since Atlanta was larger than Montgomery and more centrally located.

Throughout these months, other cities in the South were beginning to experience similar disturbances. Negroes tried in various ways to desegregate buses in Tallahassee, Atlanta, New Orleans, and Birmingham.

In Birmingham, Rev. Fred Shuttlesworth, secretary of the SCLC, was determined to end segregation once and for all, if possible. He felt that the Negroes should protest the reign of terror being conducted by the police commissioner, Eugene "Bull" Connor. This commissioner had held office for many years and all the while he had enforced rigid segregation in the city. Many Negro children had grown into adulthood fearing him for his prejudice and unjust practices.

Connor and many white people in Birmingham had closely watched the activities of Rev. King and the bus boycott in Montgomery. They warned Negro leaders not to come to Birmingham to try to desegregate buses. The NAACP had been outlawed in Birmingham and there was no organization to fight for Negro rights. The only possible help for the situation had to come from the Negro churches in the city.

Finally Rev. Shuttlesworth invited a few Negro ministers from other cities to attend a mass meeting at his church. These ministers arrived the evening before and the group worked most of the night planning a new organization to be called the Alabama Christian Movement for Human Rights. They felt that they would need an organization of this kind, especially since there was no local group of the NAACP in Birmingham to fight for Negro rights.

There also was a possibility that the new organization might have to operate in other cities in Alabama. The Negroes in all cities in the state were suffering from the same kind of inhuman treatment as in Birmingham.

On the night of the mass meeting the church was crowded with Negro men and women. They listened closely to find out about their new organization for freedom. Everyone was enthusiastic, and they elected Rev. Shuttlesworth president. It was decided that a similar mass meeting would be held every Monday night, each night at a different church in the city. The main purpose was to unite the Negroes of the city into a drive for freedom.

In the meantime matters went from bad to worse in Birmingham. Finally Rev. Shuttlesworth and his organization, the Alabama Christian Movement for Human Rights, began to fight more openly in the freedom movement. They demanded that Negroes be put on the police force, but no Negroes were hired. Then they sued the city to allow Negroes to take examinations to become policemen, but lost.

Finally Rev. Shuttlesworth and his group asked that the buses be desegregated, but no action was taken. He announced that immediately after Christmas representatives of his organization would ride in the front seats of the buses. On Christmas eve his house was bombed and a wall of his church was damaged.

On the day after Christmas, he led a large group of followers downtown to board the buses. Many of them were thrown into jail, but they paid their fines and were released. Then they filed suit to desegregate the buses of the city. Later they decided to boycott the buses, as Negroes had done in Montgomery.

Bull Connor was enraged by the boycott. He screamed, "No Negro minister can tell his people to stay off the buses."

Rev. Shuttlesworth answered this remark bravely by saying, "I'll tell my people what to do, if I have to go to prison."

Birmingham became an important center of the freedom movement. Rev. Shuttlesworth's car was seized by the State and his driver's license revoked without cause. About once a month he was jailed, first for one reason and then for another.

In 1960 the students at Miles College in Birmingham held a sit-in. Rev. Shuttlesworth joined the students, was thrown into jail and beaten. Later he encouraged Negroes to join a movement, called Freedom Ride, in which Negroes assembled in important cities of the South to demand equal rights. One important Freedom Ride was in Jackson, Mississippi, during which protesting Negroes were terrorized despite their non-violent activities.

Rev. Shuttlesworth worked far into the night to help Negroes get out of Birmingham to join the Freedom Ride movement. All the while Bull Connor was trying in every way possible to stop them. Finally after they had boarded an airplane and were safely on the way, he arrested Rev. Shuttlesworth and took him to jail.

While the Freedom Rides were under way,

Rev. Shuttlesworth left his home town and moved with his family to Cincinnati. He became pastor of a church in Cincinnati, and returned to Birmingham on weekends to fight for freedom. The Negroes in Birmingham still believed in him and he had many followers.

Early in 1962, Rev. Shuttlesworth talked with Rev. King about possible steps that could be taken to break Bull Connor's "reign of terror." "What can we do about a man that rules only by fear, not by law?" he asked Rev. King.

The two men reached no decision on possible activities, but Rev. Shuttlesworth vowed that he would never give up. "You have to be willing to die before you can begin to live," he declared. "One thing is sure, I won't give up unless they kill me."

Several months later the Southern Christian Leadership Conference came to the rescue of Rev. Shuttlesworth and his group. In September the Southern Christian Leadership Conference decided to hold an annual convention of all its eighty-five branches in Birmingham. The white business men heard about the convention, and wanted to meet with the Negroes. They formed a Committee of Senior Citizens to meet with Rev. Shuttlesworth and other Negro citizens.

During the meeting the white business men agreed to remove the Jim Crow signs in some of the stores before the convention. Rev. Shuttlesworth warned them that if the signs did not stay down after the convention was over, he would ask the Southern Christian Leadership Conference to carry out an active campaign against segregation in the city.

The Jim Crow signs were taken down for the convention, but were immediately put back up after the convention was over. Rev. King and Rev. Shuttlesworth met and decided that they should take immediate action. Rev. King promised the full support of the Southern Christian Leadership Conference and its branches.

In the meantime, Bull Connor was voted out of office, but he refused to move out, unless the court ordered him to leave. Easter was approaching, and the Southern Christian Leadership Conference decided to boycott the downtown stores. Rev. Shuttlesworth led several hundred Negro citizens to city hall to announce they would not shop in the stores for Easter. Negroes jammed the sidewalks to cheer the marchers on. Hundreds were arrested and thrown into jail.

Rev. King and Rev. Abernathy came to the city to give support to the movement. The city government obtained a court order to prevent Negroes from demonstrating. The Negroes attempted to march anyhow, and fifty of them, including Rev. King and Rev. Abernathy, were arrested and thrown into jail. Rev. Shuttlesworth was not arrested at this time, because he was busy in the community collecting money to bail persons out of jail.

While Rev. King was in jail, he thought of another kind of marching movement. This march would include children, since children, like adults, should be privileged to enjoy freedom. "The children are ready to support the movement," said Rev. Shuttlesworth.

The children's march was organized and more than a thousand children tramped slowly down the street. As they walked along, they sang, "I'll Never Turn Back No More," and other freedom songs. They meant what they said and kept on, even when the police, with police dogs and fire hoses, tried to stop them. Rev. Shuttlesworth was slammed to the ground by the force of water from a fire hose and carried away on a stretcher.

People on TV watched in horror as dogs bit children, and hoses flattened them to the pavement or drove them to the gutter. Police moved

174

in swinging clubs and savagely beating the demonstrators who kept standing, where possible, and singing freedom songs.

Bombs destroyed or tore into many buildings in the Negro area, and the people forgot to be nonviolent. They took to the streets, angry, and beat their way to the police. Finally the police sealed off the Negro area.

President John F. Kennedy sent a representative from Washingon to seek to bring peace to the community. This representative met with white and Negro committees to see what could be done. People everywhere were interested and Rev. King said, "Decent people all over the nation have joined our fight."

Gradually segregation began to give way in Birmingham. In the spring of 1963, stores were opened to Negro customers as well as white customers. Negroes were promised jobs that they never had been allowed to hold before and all the Negroes in jail were set free. Most important of all for the Negroes, Bull Connor was ruled out of office by the court.

Much violence continued in the city for several months. A bomb was exploded at a motel where Rev. King and Rev. Shuttlesworth were holding a conference. The Negroes fought back, and several people were hurt.

In the early fall, a bomb was exploded in the Sixteenth Street Baptist Church, where Rev. Shuttlesworth had been pastor. Sunday school was in session, and there were many young people in the building. Four girls were killed and several other children were injured.

While the Birmingham trouble was in progress, Rev. King and the Southern Christian Leadership Conference were involved in fights on several fronts. Students in the colleges of the South were striking out for freedom. Frequent outbreaks occurred because students were not allowed to enter restaurants, movies, churches, and other similar public places.

Several years before, an organization, called the Student Nonviolent Coordination Committee, had been organized. This organization had its headquarters in the office of the Southern Christian Leadership Conference in Atlanta. Its leaders included many prominent young Negroes of the South. Gradually the name of the organization was shortened to "Snick."

The members of Snick were taught to be nonviolent. They were taught to react to violence by not fighting back. They were taught to accept pain by practicing painful situations. Some were burned with cigarettes and some were beaten about the head and face, but they did not flinch. Some were showered with water, but they took their punishment calmly. Usually the students were housed and fed by the people in the communities where they demonstrated.

One of the chief problems in southern cities was that Negroes were not allowed to vote. They had to take tests in order to register for voting. When they attempted to register, they were kept waiting so that only a very few could be registered in a day.

The members of Snick conducted a steady campaign to register Negroes to vote. Citizenship classes were held to help Negroes understand what voting meant, and how important it was in the fight for freedom. The classes taught them how to pass the tests which they were required to pass in order to register.

In some cases, Snick volunteers moved into the rural Negro areas and lived among the people. At several places the volunteers were beaten, arrested, and jailed. One of the chief centers of opposition was in Mississippi, where a thousand volunteer students poured into the state to promote the cause of freedom to vote.

In 1965 Snick volunteers went to Selma, Alabama, to help Negroes register to vote. The local sheriff ruled the city with the same kind of fear that Connor had used in Birmingham. Many Negroes were jailed and beaten, and finally a local Negro leader was killed. News of his death spread widely.

Rev. King went to Selma to deliver a memorial address for the murdered leader, but was arrested and put in jail. Then the members of the Southern Christian Leadership Conference decided to organize a march to Montgomery, the state capital, to talk with the governor. Montgomery was fifty miles away.

Hundreds of men, women, and children gathered in the streets of the Negro section of the city. They lined up in a column, four abreast, to start their long march. Rev. King was in Atlanta when the march started, but planned to join the marchers before they reached Montgomery.

Just outside the city, where the highway led over a bridge, Alabama state troopers blocked the marchers' path and ordered them to break up. The marchers immediately dropped to their knees on the highway in prayer. The troopers filled the air with tear gas, and began to beat the marchers with whips and clubs. They chased and continued to beat the blinded, bloodied, and terrified marchers back to their homes in the city. TV cameras were trained on the marchers and the entire nation watched, shocked and stunned by the merciless treatment.

Rev. King rushed back to Selma, determined to lead a march to the state capital. He called upon ministers and others of all faiths from across the country to join him. People from everywhere, including Negroes, whites, Protestants, Catholics, and Jews, flew into Alabama to join him. Rev. Shuttlesworth brought a horde from Birmingham.

The governor obtained an order from the court, forbidding groups to assemble on the highway. Rev. King and his supporters began their march, but were stopped by the state troopers. They held a prayer service on the highway, and marched back through the streets of Selma unmolested. The Rev. King drove to Montgomery to ask that the ban be lifted.

In 1963 a civil right bill was introduced in Congress to give Negroes the right to vote without discrimination. The Negroes of the country were eager to have this bill passed and decided to organize a vast march on Washington to encourage Congress to pass the bill.

The "March" was really the dream of A. Philip Randolph, President of the Brotherhood of Sleeping Car Porters and Vice-President of the AFL-CIO Union. He called a meeting of the leaders of five important organizations of the country which were fighting for civil rights.

182

These leaders agreed to support the demonstration, which would be a mammoth affair.

During the meeting Mr. Randoph reviewed the turmoil that had existed in recent years. He recalled that in 1955 the arrest of Mrs. Parks had sparked the Montgomery bus boycott.

He pointed out that drives for integration had taken place in many southern cities, but without noteworthy improvement of Negro rights.

By 1963 demonstrations, marches, pickets, and sit-ins were being held in many cities across the nation. Mr. Randolph felt that the time had come to march on Washington, the capital of our country. This march would help Congress realize the importance of passing the civil rights bill which it was considering.

The "March" was carefully planned with more than a million persons invited to converge on the city. Every possible step was taken to avoid violence despite the fact that many persons thought that violence would occur. All persons planning to participate were carefully instructed to avoid violence in every form.

Late in August thousands of people from cities and farms across the country began to pour into Washington. They came by airplane, railroad, bus, and automobile and some even walked. One man rode a bicycle and another came on roller skates.

All kinds of people came, from all races and creeds and from all walks of life. Finally they assembled at the Lincoln Monument on both sides of the reflecting pool. For three hours they listened to speakers, who demanded passage of the civil rights bill.

Finally Rev. Martin Luther King, Jr. came before the vast crowd of people. He told them that he dreamed of a new America with equal opportunities for all. He dreamed of an America where boys and girls could move about freely,

obtain an education, and look to the future with confidence and success. He spoke eloquently as he pictured the kind of America they all hoped to have and to love.

At the end of the meeting, the people returned to their homes as quietly as they had come. Early the following year Congress passed the civil rights bill and President Lyndon B. Johnson signed it to become the law of the land. The passage of this law meant that a great step had been taken to insure equal opportunities for all, wherever they live.

"Mine Eyes Have Seen the Glory"

By this time in life, Dr. Martin Luther King, Jr. was widely known and respected. Later in 1963, after his famous speech in Washington, D. C., he was named "Man of the Year" by *TIME* magazine. In honoring him the magazine said that he had dominated the headlines of the year and profoundly influenced the nation's history.

One year later Rev. King received word that he had been awarded the Nobel Peace Prize, the second Negro ever to receive this high honor. When he received the notice, he said, "Every penny of the prize money will be donated to the civil rights movement."

Rev. King went to Oslo, Norway, to receive the award. He was accompanied by his close relatives and a host of friends. His wife, swelling with pride over his honor, said, "No matter how many honors others give him, he never forgets to give honors, too."

His father added that he was proud of him because as a boy he learned to take punishment like a man. "He has taken so much from so many people," he said.

His mother remembered that when as a teenager he had been aroused over the problems of Negroes, "He acted just as if the world was waiting for him to grow up to straighten out the problems."

Rev. Martin Luther King, Jr. in accepting the award paid great tribute to his family, particularly to his wife and parents. In closing his remarks, he said, "I will go out and give my life and my heart to all that the Nobel Peace Prize represents." Then he led everyone in the room in silent prayer.

When he returned to his home town of Atlanta, he was hailed as a great American. A special meeting was held at Morehouse College and a city-wide dinner was held downtown to honor him. At the age of thirty-four, he had become a distinguished citizen not only of Atlanta, but of the entire world.

After Rev. King received the Nobel Peace Prize, he worked even harder for the cause of freedom. He traveled to many cities, both in the North and in the South, to help fight injustices of all kinds against Negroes. His name became a symbol in non-violent efforts to bring about equal rights for citizens, regardless of their color.

In the spring of 1968 the sanitation workers of Memphis, Tennessee, most of whom were Negroes, went on strike to obtain better working conditions. In March the workers and their supporters attempted to hold a peaceful parade, which turned into a riot. The city ruled that no more demonstrations could be held.

Rev. King, Rev. Abernathy, and other members of the Southern Christian Leadership Conference decided to help the striking sanitation workers. Early in April a public meeting was held to organize another parade. Rev. King addressed the meeting, urging his listeners to avoid rioting of every sort.

In his speech Rev. King said that he couldn't foretell what would happen. He urged everyone to be unafraid, saying that he was confident, that he had reached the mountain top and had seen the promised land. He ended his address with the words, "Mine eyes have seen the glory of the coming of the Lord."

These were the last words that Rev. King ever spoke at a meeting. The next day he held conferences with a number of leaders to make final arrangements for the parade. Early that evening he walked to the balcony of his motel, still talking and planning with his friends. Then suddenly he was killed by a sniper's bullet, fired from a nearby building.

The whole country was shocked. Approximately 100,000 people, Negro and white, from all stations in life, journeyed to Atlanta to pay their last respects to this fallen leader. The services were held at the Ebenezer Baptist Church, where his father was pastor. Dr. Benjamin Mays, former president of Morehouse College and a close family friend, delivered the chief eulogy. The music included some of his favorite songs in the freedom movement, including "Ain't Got Time to Die," "Precious Lord Take My Hand," and "We Shall Overcome."

Rev. Borders summed up his notable career by saying, "In civil rights, he outstripped the world.

He died for the cause, and was killed for the cause. He was a great American."

Thus ended the life of Dr. Martin Luther King, Jr., martyr for freedom, who had sought by nonviolent means to end the last remnants of slavery in America. He had striven to break down prejudices against Negroes and to help Negroes prove themselves worthy of respect and equality. Continuously he had looked forward with confidence to the day when all men could live together in harmony and peace.